An Exotic Life

Kanda Dara

It's 10 pm on a January Saturday night in Honolulu, Hawaii.
While tourists are strolling through Waikiki enjoying the tropical
Hawaiian night air, cooled by a winter trade wind redolent with the
gentle fragrance of sampaguita flowers, the Hot Zone Exotic night
club just outside of Waikiki, is packed with men of all ages and
walks of life. All share a single focus of getting drunk and ogling
the beautiful naked women dancing on the Hot Zone stages. The
dancers are also singularly focused - to make as much money as
possible and a Saturday night like this can go a long way towards
making their rent and car payment for another month. It's not a
night for the timid, especially a timid stripper. I'm not timid.
Dancing in a small bright yellow g-string and bra, both of which
will come off many times over the course of the evening, the
elevated stage I'm on feels like a small raft floating on a sea of
testosterone, loud music, and beer fumes. Looking at the men
crowding around the stage, I can see horniness is an equal
opportunity phenomenon, knowing no social or economic
boundaries; a brotherhood of mindless lust and diminished big
brain power (as opposed to their little brains which are now totally
dictating their actions). The atmosphere is an alcohol-fueled,
hormonal-charged assault on the senses. It's a primitive
environment I struggle to ignore as I concentrate on pleasing a
young man sitting directly in front of me, my first customer of the
night. He has a big grin and plenty of dollar bills in his right hand
that I'm going to make sure end up in the garter on my left leg
before he leaves. I'm giving him all my best poses and if I'm

skillful enough in sexually arousing him, he may to go to the ATM at the back of the club to replenish his dollar bill supply at least once and possibly buy me a couple of $20 Lady's drinks. Seeing how young he is, I know getting him aroused won't be a problem. In fact, I can already see an erection straining the seams of his zipper and his eyes hypnotically fixated on my crotch, all that's missing is drool coming out of his mouth. He's just one of many customers I'll get naked for tonight, all eager to pay and pay well for the privilege of seeing my punani, which is Hawaiian for pussy. Yes, I'm a stripper, although most people will say exotic dancer because it's more artistic sounding and promises a memorable night for both local residents and tourist in a Hawaiian paradise. No matter what you call it; however, the result is the same - I get naked for money, a lot of money.

Young men, middle age men, old men, couples, and occasionally women, yes I said women, will all get an opportunity to ogle my body for as long as they keep pushing dollar bills into my garter. My bottom line is the "bottom line", *No money – No honey*….as the old Asian bargirl saying goes (or in my native Filipino language *"walang pera, walang mahal*). In other words, pay and I'll keep you entertained. After a while, the young man in front of me, my "boyfriend of the minute", will get up and move on because he's either out of money or wants to see another dancer. Either way is fine with me, someone else will take his place as soon as he leaves…and so it will go until the club closes at 2 a.m., dancing for an assembly line of customers, all with wandering hands and constant suggestions of hook ups or participation in perverted acts.... and all the while raking in the money as fast as it can be crammed into my garter belt. I have all the necessary job qualifications for success in this career, I am young, beautiful, and I have a body to die for thanks to a skilled breast augmentation surgeon, a great ass from Mother Nature, and creamy light brown skin that most women would kill for because of my Filipino heritage. All in all, if you've got it, flaunt it and profit from it...and I am showing my assets off for all they're worth to make a good living in America, the land of opportunity....and in Hawaii....paradise.

By the time the club closes, I'll have taken my clothes off and shown my precious punani to about 30-40 men, a few women, and several couples. But I'll also have about $500 - $600 in my pocket, more if I get lucky and convince some customers to pay for something other than just watching me dance. There are a range of more expensive entertainment options I'm willing to provide if the customer has the money ranging from sitting with them in a private booth while they buy me Lady's drinks, or even better, buy a more intimate one-on-one dance session in a small secluded room set off from the main dance floor (I will explain more about these other options later). Some people will say I lead a disgusting and degenerate lifestyle but really for me, it's just a job no matter how well paying it can be. I am merely taking advantage of my attractive exotic Asian looks and my youthful body. Like butterflies in the summer, my fellow dancers and I enjoy being beautiful and the center of attention but also like these same butterflies, our life-spans as attractive, sought after exotic dancers fade quickly and in only a few short years we'll be faced with the reality of having to make an honest living. This is a transition some make easily but many don't, ending up as aged prostitutes, drug addicts, or even worse trying to hang on as strippers well past their prime.

This is my story and the story of my fellow dancers. It is sometimes not a pretty tale and for most of us it will not end with a handsome prince riding in to take us away, but it is also not a tale of hopelessness and depravity. I hope it helps you understand all of us who labor away in the sex trade. We certainly don't consider ourselves perverts or sexual deviants but just working class people like everyone else. We all have normal lives outside the club - mothers, husbands/boyfriends, children, bills, and dreams of eventually leaving the stripping life. You may not like us but I hope my story will help you understand us just a little, or at worst, allow us the courtesy of casual acceptance.

Amaya

My stage name is Amaya or just Mya (pronounced Mee Yah). It's not my real name dummy, the Hot Zone manager gave it to me when I was hired. He said he wanted me to have an exotic name to match my Asian features. I didn't like it at first but it's kind of grown on me and now I prefer it to my real name - something I won't tell you so I can keep a little privacy in my life which is all too public in the first place. I won't try to candy-coat what I do for a living – I get naked for strangers, showing them parts of my body only a gynecologist should see. To be sure, it's not what I envisioned myself doing when I was young and dreaming of a career but it's what I'm doing now to make a living. To be crystal clear, it's <u>not</u> who I am; IT WON'T BE WHAT I'LL BE DOING FOR THE REST OF MY LIFE. In fact as you read my story, you'll see I'm constantly trying to quit stripping by finding other employment – all failures so far, but I keep trying. To be frank, writing this book is an attempt to get out of the stripping life; so please buy it. Ha Ha. Save a stripper, it might even be tax deductable if you have the nerve to list it on your tax return. Ha Ha.

If you were looking at me right now, you'd see just a young Filipina girl who was born poor in a rural province of the Philippines and a good Catholic girl I might add. I don't think I look like one of those hardened strippers depicted in the movies, at least I hope not. I've seen how the stripping life takes eager young girls and ages them beyond their years. Maybe retaining at least some "youth" in my looks is the key to my success even after nine years of stripping. Having a "girl next door" look is very popular with my customers. Well, having a hot body also helps... Ha Ha. So how and why did I become a stripper? That's a good question. I don't think you could have looked at me when I was a young child and said, "She's going to be a stripper one day." You couldn't have said that about me when I was a teenager either. No one can make that kind of a prediction about any child....well, I take that back, some children seem to come out of the womb destined to be strippers or are groomed for that profession by mothers who enter their daughters in Tiny Tot Beauty Pageants. But in a holistic sense, being a stripper is not usually a genetic predisposition; instead, it's a job women fall into for a variety of reasons. I probably shouldn't say women because that denotes a mature female who is probably too old to be a stripper. A more appropriate term is "girl" because young girls are the fuel the stripping profession runs on, finally spitting them out as worn out women in the end if they don't get out themselves quickly enough.

In a way, my decision to become a stripper was based on a lot of factors, economics a major one, but also my life experiences and family background. I'll discuss them in the following pages. My goal is to share a little of my life with you so you can make an informed decision about me, Amaya, as a person and not as a stripper. You may not forgive my choice of working in the Honolulu sex industry but maybe you can understand that I am just a regular girl making a living trying to support my mother, keep a roof over our heads and food on the table.

First, here are two basic facts I want to make completely clear before we go on. I AM NOT A HOOKER – never have been nor will I ever be. I can't emphasize this enough which is why I wrote that statement in all capital letters, that's my way of shouting out a point I want you to remember. If we were in the same room, I would be saying "I AM NOT A HOOKER" in a loud and forceful voice. I <u>do not</u> take money from anyone to let them use my body for sex. Working in an industry that can erode one's feeling of self-worth, my refusal to prostitute myself is the single moral strand I pride myself on clinging to. I feel nothing but pity for women who sell their bodies for sex, and there are plenty of them here in Hawaii. I will take my clothes off for money and give you a front row seat to view my private parts from every imaginable angle but that's as far as it goes. No touching and no dates for sexual purposes…period! Second, I AM NOT A SEXUAL PERVERT, so guys put away all your porn movie inspired fantasies. I am not one of the girls in those movies…again, period! There will be no letters to the editor of Penthouse that include me as the star. I DO NOT have a collection of love toys (at least not for public display Ha Ha) or a stable of studs that I can call on for nightly videotaped entertainment either singularly or in groups. I have not been in a ménage à trois or participated in any sexual fantasy games (at least not in real life….Ha Ha…Come on, everyone has those dreams!). In fact, I haven't had many lovers at all and those I've slept with

I've viewed as potential life-mates; all failures by the way. Taking my clothes off in front of legions of drooling men has kind of soured me on anyone who's had testosterone as one of his basic chemical components. You would be put off too if you've seen the stellar examples of the male species I've danced for nightly over the years. I'll talk more about them in painful detail later. Let's just say it makes me fear for mankind in general and Angels are weeping every night they watch what goes on in the Hot Zone and see what a race of people who were developed in God's image has come to.

I try very hard to keep my stripper life separated from my home life. I never tell anyone what I do for a living; it cuts down on embarrassment and allows me to lead a somewhat normal life outside of the club. I know my mother suspects but she's afraid to talk to me about it. She's seen my dancing outfits and the pad I use to kneel on stage and I'm sure she wonders about the large numbers of dollar bills I bring home every night. I can't blame her for not wanting to ask, I don't want to talk to about it either even though it's how I make enough money to support her. Telling someone you're a stripper is always met with mixed reviews, usually negative, and the reaction I generally get is pre-judgment and disgust. As proof, I bet you've already formed an opinion of me without ever having seen or talked to me, just as I've formed an opinion of you for buying and reading this book about an Asian nude dancer. Purely for academic pursuits…right? Sorry, but there are no pictures of me in the book. Ha Ha. I'll bet you haven't let your friends see you reading it. We might be, and probably are, both wrong but that's the danger of superficial judgments. All I ask is please keep your opinions (and fantasies) in check until you finish my book and maybe (hopefully) you will have a better understanding of who I really am.

As a start, you might be very surprised at how normal and mundane my life is outside of the club. I rent an apartment, take care of my mother, send money to my family in the Philippines, go to school, and shop for groceries...all normal things. And, this may surprise you even more - I just earned a Bachelor of Science degree in Information Systems (BSIT) majoring in computer security so I guess you can describe me as a bit of a nerd, a sexy looking nerd to be sure, but still a nerd. Ha Ha. I can put a BSIT after my name when I sign it, although one of my good friends said it is more likely BITCH......and then he laughs......kind of ......he's known me for a long time and has the scars to prove it...Ha Ha.

After work, I like to go dancing in the many of the nightclubs that Honolulu has to offer. To clarify, these are normal clubs with no stripping, just me dancing and socializing with people my age. It's my way of decompressing from the un-normal other half of my life and reaffirms my confidence in the human race....at least the male portion of the human race....sort of. I still have to face horny males but these are normal sex-driven young men who enjoy talking and dancing with women not paying them to get naked. It makes me feel more like a regular person just being with them and fending off their clumsy advances. I usually don't accept offers to buy me drinks but occasionally I will, if I'm in the right mood and the guy buying it is hot looking or the guy has an amusing or inventive come on line. But this is an exception to the rule. Why? Write this down girls because this will be the subject of one my test questions at the end of the book – in a guy's mind, letting him buy you a drink somehow tells him you are interested in him…and maybe, if we get to the drink stage, I probably am. But, and this is a big BUT, it is <u>way too presumptuous</u> of him to assume I feel any obligation to him just because I accepted one drink. My panties are certainly not going to get wet with lust, as most porno books say, and I am certainly not going to drag him home or out to his car for sex on the basis of this single drink. If guys would just accept this as a basic fact of life, relationships following that drink would be less forced and probably more successful. As it is, accepting a drink inevitably makes for a difficult situation when I decide to leave, either to go home or to move on to another club. His feelings will be hurt or he'll be pissed or probably both if I don't include him in my further plans for that evening. This really puzzles me; doesn't anyone have any patience anymore? In a perfect world, I'd let him buy me a drink, we'd have a few laughs and then I would go somewhere else. He would feel very comfortable about me leaving knowing we'll probably see each other again the next time I come into the club on another night and pick up where we left off. Then, if I enjoy his company, I might think about carrying it out a little further to possibly a dinner or even a relationship. But NO, it seems the young men I meet in the clubs are hardwired into thinking buying a drink is the cost of admission into a girl's bed. And that pisses me off at the whole male race. You may laugh, or think I'm an impersonal bitch, but believe me all of my rules are there because of bitter personal experiences. I think if you did a survey of all women who go into clubs, at least the attractive ones, you'd find their rules are pretty similar to mine. I'm positive that we sisters all go by the same mantra: MEN ARE STUPID, so we deal with them the best we can. If it weren't for their peckers, they'd have no female friends, and that's not even a huge advantage because artificial peckers can be easily purchased in a variety of shapes and sizes and male bullshit is not part of the purchase price. And you're guaranteed to have a climax instead of having some drunken asshole squirt his load inside you after a few seconds of grunting and then falling asleep.

So what am I looking for in a man? Good question! If you ask me directly, I may tell you I have no preferences, but I do, and my answer may vary from night to night, or from drink to drink, Ha Ha. For starters, he has to be tall – at least six foot or better; wide shoulders are always a plus. A few extra pounds are okay but no porkers; cockiness is a real turn off. White, black, and Hispanic are OK. NO Asians. I know that sounds stupid since I'm Asian but my preferences are my preferences and I grew up around Asians, so I guess I'm turned on by anything else. Also, no mouth breathers please, an IQ above room temperature is a must. I like to think I'm fairly intelligent so it would be great to be able to have some sort of an intelligent conversation, something a little north of "I'm horny, let's fuck!" The bottom line, and why I can be cocky, is I'm young and good looking so I can be as selective as I want and still not lack candidates for my attentions.

I almost always go home without a partner. I'm not a prude, just very picky and careful. As a general rule, I don't even consider the possibility of sex with a man unless I think he has the potential for a continuing relationship. Don't get me wrong, I'm not a Nun, I have my urges, and sometimes do I go out with the pure intention of hooking up. I even picked up a guy while standing in line at a Starbucks one day; for the record, it was lousy sex and there was no return engagement – I just got a little cream with my coffee. OK, bad me!! - but it's pure biologics. Again, ask all of your lady friends. Little known fact, at least by the men in this world, WOMEN GET HORNY TOO!! We're just a little more selective of who our partners are, unlike young men who I swear will fuck anything with a skirt - or late at night with thick beer goggles influencing their decision making process, they'll fuck anything remotely female not necessarily constraining themselves to the homo sapiens species. It's a good thing they're not in my native Philippines where there are homosexuals in every club called "benny boys" who look very female and very attractive, especially if they've had female hormone treatments to give them boobs. Imagine the surprised look on the face of one of the young studs that hit on me every night if he unknowingly hooks up with a benny boy only to find out when he gets down to business that his "partner" has a bigger dick then he does. Ha Ha. You know that thought just put me right out of my bad mood. Ha Ha

Anyway that's me in a quick nutshell. On those occasions when I examine my life philosophically which isn't too often, at least not sober, I know I've come a long way from being born poor in the Philippines to driving a Nissan 350Z and hitting all of the nightclubs in Honolulu. I don't think I'm doomed to be a stripper forever; at least I hope not. As I said earlier, I just received a Bachelor of Science degree in Information Systems and I hope this degree will be the springboard to get me hired into a job (or better, a career) that will pay well enough to allow me to quit the stripping profession FOREVER. IT WILL HELP ME FIND A BETTER JOB!! Think positive girl…think positive! But as the years go by and I find myself still taking my clothes off in front of strangers, I'm starting to get a little apprehensive I may never escape and I'll turn into those ancient strippers you see in every club wondering why they're still there. I lead a life I enjoy in spurts but it's also a life I'm constantly trying to escape from by any means possible.

Beginnings – Mabuhay ang Pilipinas

When I first considered telling my story, I had visions of an elaborate Hollywood production featuring flashbacks showing my humble beginnings interspersed between lurid scenes of me dancing naked before lusting men. The premise of these flashbacks would be to rationalize why I dance naked by depicting it as a predictable outcome of growing up in the poverty of a third world country, case closed. In other words, I was a victim of circumstances with only limited choices over how I lead my current life. Maybe that's true to a certain extent. I won't deny my early life wasn't a factor and I certainly can't deny the big money you can make as a stripper with no effort other than taking your clothes off was appealing, especially in view of my alternates. As a foreign national with only a basic high school education, the best I could hope for in a normal job is working for minimum wage in a convenience store or a restaurant; both of which I tried and hated. But as we all know, life isn't that simple and it certainly isn't as cut and dried as a movie plot. I didn't just wake up one morning and say to myself, gee I'm tired of being poor so I'll do anything to get money. To the contrary, I've experienced a number of milestones or decision points in my life that colored my career decisions and not all were directly related to early childhood. Plenty of other girls grow up in the same humble environment I did and don't become strippers. A lot were my high school classmates here in Honolulu. They didn't become strippers but then again, their aspirations were nothing more than finding a husband, having children, and maybe getting a minimum wage job to help make ends meet. Not for me. Sorry. I had higher life goals and probably the most correct way to summarize my decision to take my clothes off in public is as a convenient means to an end; a way to earn an income at a level I could survive on in Honolulu while I prepared for a more permanent career such as attending college and getting rich owning my own business. There is a popular saying in the Philippines: *"Walang mahirap na gawa 'pag dinaan sa tiyaga"* (Nothing's hard to do if you pursue it through perseverance.) So, if you will bear with me before we get to the juicy parts, I'd like give you a brief idea of my childhood and some of what I think are the more significant events, I call them milestones, that lead me on my path to Hell...Ha Ha. Or seriously, on my path to a lifelong career, something I am still working on and persevering to accomplish.

Ako ay ipinanganak at lumago sa aking maagang kabataan sa isang maliit na bukid bayan sa Pilipinas na tawag Sipalay (I was born and grew to my early teens in a small rural town in the Philippines called Sipalay). Have you ever heard of it? I didn't think so. It's not a major urban center in the Philippines, just a small, sleepy rural town in a remote Philippine province. According to Wikipedia, Sipalay is a "fourth class city" in the

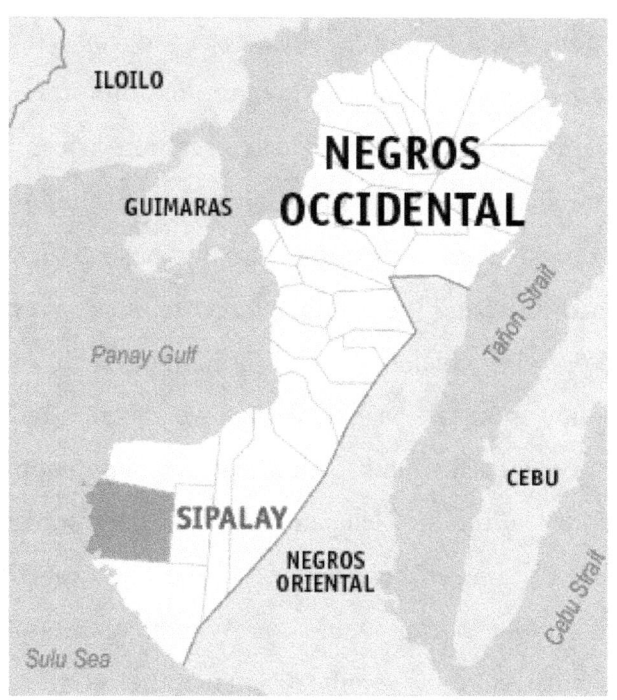

Sipalay, Philippines

province of Negros Occidental, Philippines, population in 2000 of 62,063. I was surprised at this number because my memory of Sipalay is as a very small town. I think they got that population figure by counting every little hamlet and farm in the 200 miles between Sipalay and Bocolod City. Getting to Siplalay is not easy, especially during rainy season. You have to take a 30-minute plane ride south from Manila, the capital of the Philippines, to the island of Bacolod where Sipalay is located. Then after landing, endure a grueling eight-hour bus ride reach my hometown. In other words, I grew up in a tiny little rural village in the middle of nowhere in a small third world country. I don't exaggerate when I say it's a grueling bus ride to where I grew up but then again all bus rides in the Philippines are grueling, some even kill you. It's a rare year when the newspapers don't carry three or four stories of a tragic bus accident caused by a tired driver falling asleep or failing to negotiate a sharp turn on a mountain road. Some bus trips aren't bad if you have enough money to purchase a ticket in an air conditioned bus and you don't have to share your seat with someone carrying chickens to sell in the market. If you don't have much money, you take a bus with fewer accommodations: open windows, bench seats, and loaded with as many people as the bus driver can cram into the seats and into the aisles between the seats. You would be amazed how many Filipino butts can fit on a seat a regular sized American would barely feel comfortable in. We Filipinos must have the smallest butts in the world or at least the most compressible. This is strange when you consider us Filipinas have some mighty fine booties....Ha Ha...just had to throw that in.

A lot of you probably know very little about the Philippines other than it's a small country in the Pacific Ocean. Some of you probably don't even know that. The Philippines is located just across the South China Sea from Vietnam; a geographical fact the United States military was quick to take advantage of during its conflict with Viet Nam in the 1960s and 1970s by staging their forces out of two major bases, Subic Naval Base and Clark Air Force Base. The Philippines has a strong diplomatic relationship with the U.S., a relationship that was strengthened during WWII by the sacrifice of U.S. servicemen who fought and died alongside Filipino freedom fighters to rid the Philippines of Japanese invaders. This long standing partnership and the large presence of Americans in the Philippines inevitably led to the bleed over of American culture into the Filipino lifestyle. So much so, in fact, that for a time in the early Seventies, there was a lot of popular sentiment (or hope) among the Filipinos the Philippines was going to be annexed as another U.S. state. Visions of jobs and welfare checks danced through everyone's head. After all, in certain instances, we were more American than the real Americans. Just ask the servicemen who visited the Philippines, drank our beer, loved our women – taking a lot of them home as wives. They experienced a never ending supply of nightclubs singing American music and bar girls willing to spend some quality time with them in bed after the clubs closed. There was a popular term the Americans used to describe the bar girls they encountered – Little Brown Fucking Machines (LBFMs). I find this totally objectionable and insulting, but it was true. Both Clark and Subic were considered by the U.S. servicemen as adult entertainment Disneylands, generating a lot of *mestizo* children, a number of which are popular singers and actors in the Filipino entertainment industry today. The U.S. rent for these bases, and the money spent by the servicemen on their Filipina lovers, was a major industry for my country until some nationalistic asshole politicians in our government decided they were tired of being an occupied country and asked the U.S. to leave, and oh by the way, also leave all of the infrastructure on the two bases intact. It doesn't take a genius to imagine how the U.S. government received that request. I'm thinking "What the fuck?" was asked many times.

These Filipino nationalists were all rich people and received very little benefit from the U.S. presence but it was a way of life for anyone who lived near one of the bases. I think this impasse could have been easily worked out; however, with the liberal application of money but I guess God wasn't having any of that. Right at the same time the Filipinos were telling the U.S. to leave, a large volcano on Luzon Island (near Clark AB) called Mount Pinatubo blew up covering everything in ash and mud flows. The U.S. looked at what it would cost to clean up the bases if they really wanted to stay and told the Philippine government "see yah" - leaving a big hole in the Philippine gross national income. This was the world I was born into, a much poorer Philippines. So poor in fact that one of the major industries of the Philippines is now sending workers to other countries hoping they'll send the major of their wages back to support their families still in the Philippines. The U.S. and other countries are now very stingy in granting visa to Filipinos, thinking rightly, they won't want to return to the Philippines. There are a lot of Filipinos living in the U.S. illegally right now, their visas expired and they just went into hiding.

With this backdrop, you can't help but leap to a conclusion that any Filipino immigrant coming from the poor and disadvantaged environment I grew up in has a psychological drive to make as much money as possible by any means. It's a fair point and probably a valid rationale in a lot of cases. I confess I did want to earn money, but as you'll learn later, there were also other factors. I don't think I had a strong psychological imperative to make money by any means possible because I just didn't think I was all that disadvantaged when I was growing up in the Philippines. "Disadvantaged" is such subjective terms, best considered within the context of how everyone else lives around you. If you live in a tenement and everyone else around you lives in luxury apartments then you know you are disadvantaged. Conversely, if you are poor and all your relatives and neighbors are likewise just as poor....well...different story. Granted, we had very little money and had to scramble for what we had but so did everybody else. Everyone lived in poorly constructed one or two room shacks, a lot had no running water or electricity. My home had no electricity for quite a while in my young life. I had very little clothing, just a couple of raggedy dresses, well-worn panties and flip flops...just like all of my friends. On the positive side, at least I <u>did</u> have panties...a lot of young children just ran around naked, still do. You don't need much else in a tropical climate. Everyone in my family, from the oldest to the youngest, parents and children, was expected to do their part to make ends meet. We were no better or worse off than our neighbors but we had a roof over our heads and food on the table every night, however humble it all was. Below is a picture of a Filipino house similar to the one I grew up in. Although it wasn't much, at least it was partially constructed using concrete blocks making it considerably sturdier than a lot of the nipa huts (*bahay kubo)* used by the very poor that are constructed of nothing more than bamboo with and thatched "nipa/anahaw" leaves. These houses are easily crushed when typhoons hit, a frequent occurrence during rainy season (May-November). Think U.S. trailer parks vs tornados.

A House Similar to Mine in the Philippines

The strong Filipino family culture helped soften the blow of our supposed monetary shortcomings. We were a complete family unit with a mother, father and four children. In addition to this immediate family core, there was an extended family of aunts, uncles, and cousins helping each other and expecting help in return for the common family good. This is especially true if someone makes good, such as a daughter marrying an American which is somewhat akin winning the lottery in the U.S. Once married, the daughter is expected to routinely send money to cover family living expenses and emergencies. Americans or other nationalities who marry a Filipina often have problems with this extended family concept – "You marry the girl, you marry the family." Most get over their initial shock and find out what a loving wife a Filipina can be…others divorce quickly and quietly and move on to a less family oriented spouse. This dependency on the children to support the parents is another reason for families having lots of children – they are literally breeding their own Social Security plan; the more children, the better the retirement. Children, and subsequently, their children, and the income they'll make as adults are counted on as being there to sustain the older generations long after their working years are finished. Actually, another primary reason for the large number of children you see in any Filipino neighborhood is directly attributable to the ban on birth control by the Catholic Church, an institution thrust on Filipinos during the seventeenth century Spanish occupation of the Philippines. In this, the Philippines has much in common with South America. My family had only four children which gave us a distinct financial advantage over our neighbors, fewer mouths to feed on a limited budget. Families with a dozen or more children are not uncommon. I think it's ironic that the same Catholic priests who preach against birth control can't ever marry or have children, so how in Hell can they possibly have any concept of what a burden unplanned children are to poor families. Large numbers of children simply overwhelm the limited abilities of poor families to keep food on the table or send their children to school with even the most rudimentary clothing and school supplies. The equally poor communities these families live in cannot offer any support because of their own fiscal constraints. I think my disagreeing with Catholic Church doctrine has just entitled me to a one-way, express ride to the Hell envisioned by the Church. I know my Mother, Catholic to the core, would be scandalized by my heretical views. Oh well, I'll have good company in Hell. I'll probably be seeing you all there along with child molesting Catholic priests, several Popes, and the entire order of the Dominican Friars who took great pleasures in torturing "sinners" during the Inquisitions of the Middle Ages. Anyway, my disagreement with the Church is the least of my sins. The Church aside, one other factor contributing to the large number of children is the long nights in the rural Philippine provinces with nothing much to do other than drink and have sex and the fact that we Filipinos are a romantic people at heart. Just look at our TV shows and comic books, all feature drama and romance.

Aside from the family circle, there was also a community social network supporting us, something you no longer see in the United States where each house in a neighborhood is an independent kingdom. Each family in my neighborhood knew everything about their neighbors, gossiped about each other, looked out for each other, and more importantly shared whatever limited resources they had. In other words, our neighborhood was also part of our extended family, caring and mutually supportive. I've talked to Filipinos just after they moved to America and their first impressions match mine with regards to our U.S. neighborhoods. They are amazed at how isolated everyone one is with even next door neighbors barely knowing each other beyond a brief, occasional nod of recognition or a "hello." No communal gossiping (*chismis*) during the cool of the evening, no strolling down the road saying hello to everyone.

I am the youngest of the four children in my family or in my Filipino language, the "*bunso*." My parents had their children in two widely separated groups for some reason, first my oldest brother and sister and then after a gap of several years, my next oldest brother and me. In essence, since my parents and my oldest brother and sister were busy trying to scratch out a living, my closest family interaction was limited to my other brother, Ulysses or Uly, who is only two years older than me. Being the youngest, Uly and I always had a full list of daily chores such as taking care of our family carabao (no, I didn't misspell caribou, a carabao is a domesticated water buffalo in the Philippines used for all of the heavy lifting and plowing chores), planting rice each spring, collecting eggs from our chickens to sell in the market, and running a small stall in the town market to sell whatever we could grow or make. Even though we were young, we did our chores to the best of our ability because it was expected for the good of the family as a whole. I like to think in this aspect we were much more mature and responsible than children our age in the U.S. because so much more was expected of us. However, we were still young and sometimes mistakes happened such as broken eggs; chores left undone; or in one instance, the carabao almost dying due to overheating because I (oops I meant we) wanted to play instead; or truth be told sometimes we were just not paying attention to our responsibilities. Come on, we were little children, give us a break! Except for the carabao incident which I'll tell you about in a minute, most of our transgressions were small and inconsequential (at least from the perspective of looking back at them from a distance of many years). But we weren't in the U.S., we were the Philippines where our family survival depended on the small chores we were assigned. As a consequence, any transgression, no matter how minor, always drew the wrath of my Mom – 4 foot and 5 inches of absolute terror. How tough was she? I saw her face down a large drunk man wielding a machete who was trying to kill my father. He walked away from the encounter mumbling to himself, something I frequently do even now after having a confrontation with her. She tolerated no mistakes from anyone, not even my Dad, and there was no forgiveness or letting us off with a warning. If we did screw up, we got whipped…period…end of story. They weren't selective whippings either, i.e. only the guilty got punished. Everyone felt the fallout of the explosion. Mom's philosophy was if one of us screwed up we both got whipped ….HARD, or we were subjected to a range of other punishments such as being locked in a closet. I'm sure she felt this was an efficient process…it sure saved her time that would normally be lost weeding through repeated choruses of "not me" to find out who the actual culprit was. It also gained her an extra set of eyes. If I saw my brother doing evil, you can bet I would tear into him to stop so I wouldn't get whipped too when Mom found out what he did…and she would find out because my brother was stupid. It was scary how she always knew. You could probably call it child abuse looking at it from the politically correct societal perspective of the U.S., but that certainly wasn't a view shared in the neighborhood where I grew up. Here a certain level of physical discipline was expected and rigorously practiced (spare the rod and spoil the child). I didn't see any of my neighborhood friends being treated differently. If the punishment wasn't carried out by my Mother or Father, it was most certainly enforced by my Grandmother, "*Lola*" in my language. If you've never been to the Philippines and want to envision a typical *Lola*, just think of a wizened, stooped little old lady, gray hair, about five foot nothing weighing less than 80 pounds and tough as a rawhide strap by years of hard work the hot tropical sun. Think of a piece of dried pemmican with arms and legs. It's not unusual to see a number of *Lolas* squatting on their haunches on the side of a road gossiping with each other and smoking small, skinny cigarillos by holding the lit ends in their mouths. They have zero toleration for frivolity, deviation from the norm, and non-attendance at Mass. We children were afraid of them; hell, the adults were afraid of them. Parents would tell their children to behave or face *Lola's* wrath. I often think that will be my fate in the end, to be a *Lola* feared by all. I'm not sure I'll ever have any kids of my own, but I'll sure terrorize all of my nieces and nephews….and their parents. Ha Ha.

My father was a good man, gentle with good intentions, but he was too weak and easily dominated by my Mom. Despite this, he did his best to protect us from her punishments and in fact saved us from whippings on more than one occasion by admitting to doing the wrong we were guilty of. I loved my Father. He died when I was nine years old, way too early for me to lose such an important figure in my life. I often tear up when I see his picture because I still miss him very much and think how nice it would have been to have had him in my life while growing up. Maybe my life would be a lot calmer than it is right now and probably not as interesting, certainly not interesting enough to write a book about. I know for a fact it wouldn't have been as stressful.

Looking back from the perspective of being an adult now, I can kind of understand my Mom's behavior with respect to not letting us be children. As I said, our family's livelihood was at stake and it demanded a high level of participation from everyone in the family so we could eat on a regular basis and keep a roof over our heads. I can understand it, but I will never overlook her cruelty and I will NEVER FULLY FORGIVE HER FOR THAT CRUELTY. One of my most traumatic childhood memories took place when I was seven; you might even call it my first life milestone. I had come home early from school feeling really sick and all I wanted was a little TLC from her. Isn't that what Moms do, give you TLC when you need it? She wasn't having any of that. She quickly (and coldly I might add) pushed me away telling me to leave her alone. Again looking back on this I can see this rejection somewhat from her viewpoint, she was too busy to take care of my small problem, but then another part of me says she could have spared a couple of minutes to coddle me and make me feel better. I cite this small incident as the progenitor of my hard shelled personality. I vowed right then and there never to rely on anyone ever again and began keeping an emotional distance from everyone, no matter how close they are to me, so I would never be hurt by rejection. It's a pretty adult emotion for someone so young, but it helped me mentally survive my Mom even though she was physically beating me. I still have this shell around me and it's served me well over the years, making me tough and resilient. It sure helps me keep emotionally detached while dancing. OK....I'm a cold bitch...get over it...it helps me survive. On the downside; however, it also prevents me from finding love by not allowing anyone into my heart and inner feelings, or allowing me to extend myself to someone else. I've heard the term emotional frigidity before, and maybe that's me. More than a few potential life mates have been discouraged because I couldn't express my feelings of love to them or let them fully into my life. I'm not even sure I know what love is. I have a good friend who says I have three levels of identity (I'd say personalities, but that would make me sound crazy...Sybil?). He calls my professional dancer personality the first level - my Amaya level. This is my hard outer shell, an emotionally detached professional demeanor I use to cope with being nude in front of customers every night in the club. Amaya lets me compartment and forget everything I encounter at work. This is the part of me that surfaces whenever I meet someone new or there is something unpleasant going on in my life. If someone offends me, it's Amaya that will never talk to them or answer phone calls from them again, ever, no mercy or second chances. Going a little deeper is another layer, my Mariel or Mari (Mar'ee) level. Mariel is the name my friends and acquaintances call me. It's the name I give to anyone who asks outside of the strip bar environment, such as when I go bar hopping. One of the reasons for using this second false name is I don't like my real name. A second is it's another layer of anonymity I take comfort in. Come on, I make my living naked, so give me a little slack when it comes to wanting to maintain some little semblance of privacy. What little privacy I have is precious to me. If I react to you on the Mari level, you've breached my professional outer defense and I consider you a friend. But don't be mislead that there is a large level of emotional commitment here either, you're a friend, but I don't consider you as an intimate or family; it would take very little for me to oust you back out to Amaya who'll forget you. Finally, there is my innermost name, my real name that I only use within the confines of my family and on legal documents. You will never see it in this book. It is my most sensitive personal level, the one closest to my emotions. Again, the good friend I continually refer to in this book is very good at getting through to this level where I don't have a lot of defenses. Even though he's not physically part of my immediate family, I consider him as such. He knows all my triggers, most of which are based in my childhood and can make me cry at will. He says it's very cathartic for me to abandon both Amaya and Mari and cry occasionally to release tension. Bastard! I'll be sitting with him in the club, and if we're having a little disagreement, I just know that he'll go right to my inner level triggers to get me emotional, or more emotional than I already am. I know he's doing it, while he's doing it, and I still let him go there for some reason. Maybe I agree with him that I do need to blow some steam every once in a while. I'm sure it's a sight my waiters wonder about, hard Amaya crying. The bouncers never even bother to look up; they're used to the drama when my friend sits with me and know the storm will soon blow over, and it does. But he can be a bastard for doing it. I'm going to talk more about this asshole friend of mine later under Sugar Daddy. What is a Sugar Daddy? Just read on Dude.

Anyway to get back to the subject at hand, in a partial defense of my Mom, she treated us the way she was treated as a child, in fact her treatment was worse, so I guess in her estimate she was being lenient with us. Mom told me how her mother would often put her or her brothers into a sack hung on a tree when they misbehaved and then beat the sack with a big stick. Although I haven't asked, I'm pretty sure this cruel discipline was handed down in my family from generation to generation; each succeeding generation never modifying it because they were uneducated and simply didn't know better or cared. A hard life demanded hard discipline. Enlightened parenting is a phenomenon of rich cultures that don't worry about day-to-day existence. As I said, in my family, the focus was surviving and any transgression that threatened our family's viability, no matter how innocent, couldn't be tolerated. On a lighter side (I guess you can see a lighter side in anything), because punishment was so severe and children will be children, my brother and I often hoarded knowledge of each other's transgressions that Mom didn't know about to use as blackmail against each other. Remember the carabao? It was me that almost killed him due to inattentiveness. One of my jobs was to take him down to the river to bathe each day to keep him from overheating and dying in the hot Filipino climate. He was a large animal and overheated easily. I was pretty reliable about doing this ......usually; however, one day I forgot about him while I was playing. When I finally remembered, he was very close to collapsing of heat stroke before I finally got him into the cool water. His death would have been a disaster because in poor families such as ours, the carabao is the center of the family's wealth and is totally essential for plowing our rice fields. But the carabao recovered nicely once I got him cooled down. It shouldn't have been a further problem, with me quietly learning a life lesson of future diligence in this critical task. But I was wrong. The problem: Uly found out about it and has never failed to use it as leverage whenever he wants something from me. A bigger problem, my mother still doesn't know about it and my brother still uses it. In fact he used it just last month to ask for money and we're both over 30. Damn!! So you ask: what transgressions did I have on my brother to blackmail him in return? Certainly nothing as serious as almost killing our carabao, but he did manage to drop a day's take worth of eggs one morning when he was in too much of a hurry collecting them from our chickens. Did he get whipped? No, thank God, because I would have been whipped too!! Instead, my father told Mom he broke them and then took a verbal lashing. Regardless, the egg incident is sometimes very useful for me to recall in my brother's presence from time to time when he is being particularly obnoxious.

I said earlier I didn't consider the conditions I grew up in as poor or disadvantaged; in fact, we had a decided advantage over our neighbors. You see, my Mom is a U.S. citizen, as was her mother. Both had lived in Hawaii to help harvest sugar cane. My Mom moved back to the Philippines in 1977 because she missed living there and had me in 1979. This was a significant factor that is still influencing my present life. If my Mom had remained in Hawaii, I would have been born a U.S. citizen under completely different social circumstances than the Philippines. I'm sure a lot of my perceptions about life would have been different. I may have even turned out like my brainless classmates in high school - marrying early and having lots of kids. But that's all water under the bridge; I WAS born in the Philippines and lived there until I was 17. The problem? My Mom didn't realize she needed to register me as a U.S. citizen born abroad before my 17th birthday. If she had done so, I would be a U.S. citizen now; but she didn't and I'm not. FUCK! But to counter the "what could have been" of my Mom staying in Hawaii, one of the few positive contributions she had in my life was deciding to move back to Hawaii in 1996. In this, I'm forced to tip my hat to her. She was poor and basically uneducated so her decision to take a long airline flight back to Honolulu, bringing my brother and I along, had to have been a hard one. It was certainly a major leap of faith into the unknown for her, and to give her credit, very courageous. Why did she decide to go? I don't know, I was a kid and she didn't share any thoughts or ideas with me, a reticence she still practices to this day. One day she left our house in Sipalay without telling me where she was going, stayed gone for what seemed forever, and then returned telling me and Uly to pack all our things because we were leaving the first thing in the morning. She didn't say where we were going but I had this funny feeling I wouldn't be coming back to Sipalay for a very long time, possibly never. So, that night I cried as I packed but there really wasn't a lot to pack, I didn't have much - at the most a pair of slippers; a couple of worn out hand me down dresses; one pair of pants; and a couple of hand-me-down t-shirts with holes that had been repeatedly repaired. I remember I continued to cry long into the night after I finished packing. I thought my world was coming to an end. But life, being the unforgiving bastard that it is, carried on despite my misgivings and we arrived in Manila two days later and in Hawaii a few days after that, on April 23, 1996 to be exact. Like a dream, I found myself exiting Honolulu Airport and stepping into a whole new world and a whole new life.

Honolulu, Hawaii – My 'Hood'

Waikiki, Hawaii, where I live now…jealous?

My arrival in Hawaii is really where my story begins. I think my early experiences here are significant causative roots to my eventual decision to become a stripper, excuse me, exotic dancer. I was 17 when I got here. Naïve, inexperienced, scared, and shy are all good adjectives to describe my introduction into American culture. I was also going through the angst of being a teenager which added fuel to the fire. OK, maybe I'm getting a little melodramatic in describing how traumatized I was. I was shocked and a little overwhelmed, yes, most people would be after moving from a very rustic rural environment into a big city, but my acclimatization was a little more gradual than what you would expect. Like most immigrants, my Mom headed straight for an environment she would be comfortable in, a Filipino neighborhood; there are many in Hawaii and she chose Kalihi where the Filipino national language of Tagalog is spoken along with a number of other native Philippine dialects. This helped eased my transition quite a bit. Other factors also helped. First, as alien as the American culture can be to immigrants, it is not overwhelming to Filipinos because, as I said earlier, Americana permeates every corner of the Philippines. Second, English is a common second language for all Filipinos and is taught in every school. Thanks to this, I could speak a little English but it certainly wasn't at the level needed to succeed in high school. The English I had learned was English being taught by teachers who barely understood the grammatical basics themselves. Colloquial English gave me a lot of problems, Hawaiian Pidgin was a certifiable nightmare. (*Hey Brah! You like beef? (You want to fight?).* But no matter the advantages I had in integrating into my new American life from a language perspective, there was one serious problem that may have been a major reason for my first foray into the stripping profession. From my very first day of school, the American values I began picking up, especially those practiced by my school friends clashed with the still prevalent Filipino culture my Mom expected me to live up to. This is a common problem for all immigrant children, some cope, I had problems, and I eventually rebelled, looking for any means to escape my Mother.

My first two years of high school, grades 10 and the 11, were pretty tame. I was a good daughter or at least a subdued daughter, uncorrupted and trying hard to succeed in school. That was only because Mom was still very strict, treating me exactly like she did in the Philippines, you know, beatings when I messed up, but I've already told you about that. She would also launch into morality lectures on sex whenever she saw a young pregnant teenager or a young teenage girl pushing a stroller, both frequent sights in Kalihi. It became a weekly catechism for me: "See? That will be you if you mess up and then your life will be ruined and your family will be ashamed of you!" I honestly felt degraded. I mean, how the hell could she tell me I'll turn out exactly like those children (not women) who have babies before they can even get a job? I wanted to tell my Mom in no uncertain terms, "Do I really look that stupid to you?" And on top of that, I didn't even have a freaking boyfriend! But, I was still young and inexperienced in American society, so I just endured her rants the same way I did when I was in the Philippines, I crawled into my shell. I say I endured but that doesn't mean I was content in accepting it; I was also changing, maturing. During my senior year, I started making friends and when I noticed how they were treated at home, no beatings and much more understanding, I began to talk back to my Mother. I know you can see the disaster coming, a young impressionable girl just starting to get her Americanized feet under her and an intractable mother who couldn't even begin to understand those changes.

There were a lot of Filipino girls my age in my school. Most were native Tagalog speakers; even better, some could even speak my local dialect of Visayan. Although this helped to ease my transition into American school life, I guess in a spurt of young wisdom, I began to see that for me to succeed in this country, I needed to speak and understand English better than I did at that point, better then my friends did. I didn't want a heavy Filipino accent muddying what I was trying to say in English or a Tagalog language filter slowing down my understanding of English because I would first have to translate everything I heard or read from English into Tagalog before reacting. So, I started hanging out with non-Filipinos, improving my English skills through immersion into their discussions and exchanges of ideas. This drew the wrath of my Filipino friends, but I didn't care. At that point, I was beginning to develop the stubborn independent streak that has served me well over the years. I analyze a problem and then take immediate, direct actions to fix it, no matter what anyone thinks. I guess it was also a part of my rebellion against my mother to more fully break out of the Filipino culture. No matter what caused my actions, it worked. Now my friends say I have no accent at all while their English is still very heavily "Filipino-ized". We're still friends, don't get me wrong, and I still see them from time to time; however, they're still entrenched in their isolated Filipino communities while I've broadened my horizons to become more metropolitan. I live, work, and play in the big city. Besides my high school friends, I also began to have older, college student friends that I met working on my first job after school, a cheap buffet restaurant in Waikiki. Definitely not a job I would envision as a permanent career choice but a typical teenage first attempt at employment. Anyhow, my college student coworkers would invite me to go out after work and just hang out somewhere with them. We weren't doing anything wrong, we certainly didn't do any alcohol or illegal drugs that most parents, my Mom in particular, torture themselves to death thinking their children are involved in. Well, not much alcohol, we were young so give us a break. We would mostly just hang out in somebody's house till three or four in the morning and then I would get dropped off at home. I know, I know, you can see the thunderclouds forming and the storm rolling in....and it did....*drum roll please*. The third time I came home late, my mother warned me if I ever did it again she would shave off all my hair so I would be too ashamed to have a social life. I remember thinking she would never do such thing. WRONG!! Shortly thereafter, I came home very late for the fourth time. Remember, I was in a state of rebellion. I quietly snuck into the one room my Mom and I shared and since the light was off I thought "good, she's sleeping" and slowly crawled into bed. Just when I was ready to fall asleep, the light suddenly came on and the next thing I heard was the sound of the electric shaver coming towards my head. Panicked, I jumped out of bed and somehow managed to get out of the room and into in the street with my hair still intact. Not a good move in Kalihi Valley at night. It was cold and rainy and I only had on my night clothes. I wanted to run away from that crazy woman but I was still in high school and really had nowhere to go. So, I went back into the house and took my beating and the degrading lectures one more time. Although I avoided getting my head shaved, that night was different and was another one of those milestones that happen in everyone's life. I promised myself I would get my own place to live soon as I graduated from high school and get the hell away from my mother. My mother apparently also shared those feelings, probably to no one's surprise who has ever had teenage daughters. I remember telling her to just wait until I finished high school and then she would never have to put up with me any longer. Her response? "GOOD." A few short months before high school graduation, I got my first opportunity to make a break, but it didn't come in the form of a new apartment. It came via a husband, Mark. Yes, I got married!

Who Needs a Husband?

I've been married…TWICE as a matter of fact…with several near misses on future ex-husband number three. I want to briefly cover these attempts at marital bliss because they're an important part of my story, and I want to prove I'm not the stereotypical cold, heartless stripper bitch you see in the movies…or are probably picturing me as. I also think had I persevered in either one of these marriages, I wouldn't be stripping now. I went into each bright-eyed and full of hope, only to fail miserably. I really don't know what went wrong. Maybe my expectations were too high, or more probably I'm just not cut out for married life. I do know if I acquire another husband, he'll have to be a 'saint" to survive all of the cynicism I've built up over the years. Although this cynicism has served me well at times and, as I mentioned earlier, gives me the protective shell necessary to survive as a stripper, it has also made it difficult to actually finding a truly nurturing relationship too. The right man could come along tomorrow, and probably has several times in the past, only to be discouraged from even trying to connect to me because of my smart mouth and hard shell. But I haven't given up trying; I have a "sort of" boyfriend now after kicking one to the curb a few months ago. I'm just not sure I'll ever really be happy within the confines of a marriage and I REALLY DON'T WANT A THIRD EX-HUSBAND. Why? What kind of impression would that give someone when they find out you have three ex-husbands? If it were another potential suitor, maybe even the Mr. Right I've been waiting for all my life, he'd be out the door before it even had a chance to hit him in the ass. Ha Ha. Anyway, I think as I grow older, and hopefully richer, I'll just "rent" love for a short period of time just satisfy an itch and then get rid of this temporary partner with no strings attached. What? Men do it all the time, even married men. So why not a woman? Maybe I'm prematurely turning into a cougar. As Tina Turner sang, "*What's Love Got to Do With It*"? You go Girl!!

Of my two trips to the altar, I think my first marriage is the most painful to write about. It certainly hurts to think about it, but it's a significant part of my story and a major departure point for my journey into life's big adventure. Mark was a U.S. Marine stationed at Kaneohe Marine Corps Base, on the east coast of Hawaii. He was young, only 23, and I was <u>very young</u> at 18. And yes, before you ask, I admit I saw him as a way to escape my Mom. Looking back; however, I'd like to think there was love between us. At least there was love on his part. He was very handsome and treated me good … and I really wanted to be a good wife. Certainly, the sex was great, and since we were young…frequent and vigorous. Right after we got married, we were able to obtain military housing on base which considerably cut down on expenses, a good thing given our limited income. Life was good ….and then I got pregnant (remember the frequent sex?). I should have been happy. I know he would have been…. <u>if I had told him</u>, but I didn't. That was stupid, I admit it, but as I said, I was very young and very scared and I didn't really have the benefit of an understanding mother to go to for advice. So I did one of the worst things I've ever done in my life - I had an abortion without telling him. I know... I know...I went from stupid to STUPID! Even after all these years, I still regret aborting my baby. My son (yes, it was a boy) would be 12 now and I think about what it would be like having a child to love and take care of, especially when I see my friends with their children. At the time, I was worried about how I was going to take care of him and I let those doubts cloud my judgment. The only example I had of motherhood was my mother, not a very good example. Maybe I made the right decision for me at that time, but it still doesn't feel right, particularly in hindsight. But I did it, and he found out ... after the fact...and that was the end. To this day, I really don't know why I didn't tell him I was pregnant right from the start and then work through a decision about what to do together...you know...like a married couple. I realize now it was a mistake, but as I said, I was young and scared, and maybe I still didn't trust him – remember my shell? Needless to say, it rocked our young marriage to the core. To say he was very angry at me is an understatement. Mark was from the bible-belt in Ohio and this went against everything he'd been taught growing up and he wanted children. I'm not going to go into any more detail other than to say I basically pulled the plug on our young marriage. Mark got orders to transfer shortly thereafter....I didn't go with him. He kept writing me for a long time asking me to follow him, but I couldn't. His mother even called me several times begging me to join Mark because he was heartbroken. I think the fact he didn't just abandon me right after he'd found out what I'd done speaks volumes for how good of a man he was, and how shallow I was not to see it. I think the fact I'm only able to come up with just a few words to describe our marriage gives you an idea about how brief it was. It's probably something I could have made work if I had been a little smarter and more experienced (or maybe more mature is a better way to put it), but that's ancient history now and I had other mistakes on my life's agenda to make.

Life after Mark was a muddle of low paying jobs and just trying to get by. I had a small apartment and not much more. I was also going to a small community college near where I live. At no time, did I ever consider moving back in with my Mom. I'm not sure she would have taken me back anyway; the wounds were still too fresh in both our minds. To my credit, I didn't see this as lost time in the story of my life where I was treading water until I could meet another husband. That's not me. I take my hits and move on with my life, and I was moving on, just husbandless. I've always had this independent streak, always have and always will. I'm not afraid of being by myself or try new things. I guess this is one of the few benefits of growing up under tough home conditions, I learned not to count on anyone but myself (the tough shell and all). In this, I suspect I have more than a little male testosterone floating around in me. All of my female friends are clingers. They need that strong male presence to get by both emotionally and financially. They have one plan in life, Plan A, in which they'll meet Mr. Right, get married, and have a house full of children.

Losing a husband would devastate them. That's not me. You will see me pound on this same theme time after time in this book: having a Plan A is good, but you also need a Plan B, C, D, etc. Plan A's only work out in the movies, not in real life. You have to be flexible and anticipate the worse and when it happens, as it always does in real life, be ready to react and adapt. No, after Mark, I wasn't moping around waiting to meet another Mr. Right. In fact, I doubted there would be another Mr. Right, or even a Mr. "He'll Do If I Lower My Standards", or a Mr. "He Might Be OK After I Work With Him For a While." Ha Ha. Little did I know at the time, I was on the track to meet someone else, not Mr. Right apparently because he turned into another ex- husband, but again I started out life with him with good intentions and a desire to make it as a wife and mother. His name was Thomas.

I met Thomas under different circumstances than Mark. I was more worldly and mature when Thomas came into my life; in fact, I was already dancing in my first exotic night club. I'll talk more about that later. Thomas was a customer who later became my husband. In a way, our early relationship was a little strange. I lived with him for a year before we finally got married in a big wedding and all of his family present. He was about 15 years older than me and very well off financially; I drove a Jaguar, so what does that tell you? Looking back, I realize that I did love him (shut up, I know what you're thinking – me, shell girl loving someone?), and for a while we were very happy, at least we had a picture-book marriage by all appearances. I can show you the wedding pictures.

We lived in a nice house and drove nice cars. We also had two cockatoos as our children, Romeo and Juliet; I still miss them. Anyway, as happens in most marriages, life began to intrude into Eden and rough spots started cropping up – differences of opinion, damaged egos, clashes in lifestyles, and we were both too immature to handle them correctly. I was still too young and although he was older, as I said, this was his first marriage, so neither of us really knew how to compromise or really live as a couple. Sometimes I felt we were just roommates rather than a married couple. This "disunity" did not give us the proper base to overcome serious problems or conflict. Our fights became epic, usually ending up with one of us doing material damage to the other's personal possessions. He didn't beat me or abuse me … but he vented his anger in other ways. He ripped up my passport for one thing and trashed a lot of my makeup so I wouldn't go out. I, on the other hand, took a higher road and flushed my wedding ring down the toilet during one argument.

Reflecting back on our marriage, I can point to three major contributors to our unhappiness. A significant one was my insistence on continuing to strip to make extra money. Although Thomas took care of my basic needs of food and shelter, I was too shy to ask him for money for clothes, makeup, manicures, etc. In hindsight, I know he would have given me as much money as I needed, if I had only asked. I know, I know, stupid me; I told you I was immature. And as I've told you before, I have this damn streak of independence that makes it impossible for me to be totally reliant on anyone. My continuing to get naked for other men was a serious blow to Thomas's ego and made him constantly jealous. In his mind, I was having sex with all my customers. I wasn't, I promise, but he thought so. Another problem, and something that still upsets me, was his reluctance go traveling with me, you know, get off the island (and off his butt) and visit other places. He always refused, saying it would be bad for his business to take time off. I really wanted him to go to the Philippines and meet my family. He never did. Eventually, I began to tire of his "stay-at-home'itis" and began taking trips by myself or with friends. The passport tearing incident came during an argument we had after I returned from a trip to New Orleans. I had gone with some friends, including some male friends. Again I promise, nothing happened, I have movies of the trip to prove that, but he was furious. Lastly, and I think most damaging, he refused to consider me as a person with goals and ambitions. I guess it stemmed from his Italian background; he was raised to consider a woman as nothing more than someone to keep your house clean, warm your bed, and have your children. He never encouraged me or helped me continue with my schooling to prepare for a profession. I think in his mind, he wondered about the need of having an educated wife, after all, he made enough money to keep us comfortable. But, I knew I was blessed with an active mind and a strong urge to realize my potential, no matter what. I was capable of being more than a stay-at-home wife and a baby machine and I let my frustrations be known. Remember my independent streak?

To make a long story short, we eventually divorced in 2004 after only two years of marriage. I still talk to him occasionally and guess what I found out? He goes to the Philippines quite frequently now. Why couldn't the Son of a Bitch have done that when we were married? I guess he's trying to find a replacement for me! I can tell him right now, it can't be done. Ha Ha. I think I'm unique...or at least my friends tell me they've never seen anyone like me...I think that's a compliment and they mean it in a good way....of course they do! Ha Ha.

As I said, I've been close to marrying a third husband several times, but haven't pulled the trigger for a number of reasons, not wanting to be known as a woman who's had three husbands is chief among them. Once burned, twice shy...and three times...stupid. My most recent adventure in stupid land was having a steady relationship with a local guy over the last year, I even lived with him. But I could tell we really had no future together, he was way too jealous for one thing. So I kicked him to the curb a couple of months ago. Now I'm seeing someone else who probably won't progress much beyond just having someone for sex. Pretty sad huh? Once I get rid of him, I'm not sure what my future will hold. Partying every night and drinking until I can't stay vertical? Or maybe I'll hook up with yet another candidate for husband number three. I said with a straight face and an optimistic feeling. Yeah, right...

My First Job as a Stripper

We're finally in one of the parts of my story you probably bought the book for, talking about my stripping life. My stripping career actually has two parts, an early job in a sperm soaked dive where I learned the profession (apprentice stripper? Ha Ha), and my current job as a seasoned professional. I hope it doesn't disappoint.

One of the problems of living on your own in Hawaii is it takes money, something I didn't have an abundance of when I broke away from my first husband. I was trying to do the right thing by going to college but it was an expensive undertaking when I barely had enough money to pay my rent and then eat on top of that. I also had a very rigid bottom line that made my life a little more difficult, I was not going to move back in with my Mom under any circumstances. I'm not even sure I had that option anyway given the hostility of our relationship at the time. She probably would have caved and allowed me to move back because she was my mother after all, but both of our lives would have been miserable and probably unbearable. Being Filipino, my Mom would have certainly made it a large drama and truthfully I would have too, remember I'm Filipino too and drama is in our DNA. I also really didn't want to admit to her I wasn't capable of living on my own...that I wasn't as adult as I thought I was. I think you can see another one of my life milestones coming. As luck would have it (or looking back reflectively, bad luck), I had a close friend, Michelle, an attractive Filipina, who I met in one of my college classes. She, like me, was trying to make it on her own because of problems at home; however, instead of working minimum wage jobs and struggling to make ends meet, she chose a different path. I still remember with crystal clarity the fateful conversation we had one day before class. I was complaining about all of the bills I had coming due with no money to pay for them. Her response was something I would have never expected. She told me she knew a way to make a lot of money with very little effort and that I should try it. Given that my bills were closing in on me, I said OK…what is it? She said STRIPPING, and this is where my true story starts. If this was a TV show, there would be a cut to a commercial with music fading in to increase the drama and then the show resumes with a tight focus shot of the shocked look on my face as I reacted to Michelle's suggestion. Michelle, it seems without me being aware of it, was an exotic dancer in one of the lower class clubs in Honolulu. I would like to say I strongly resisted the temptation for this "easy money" and said NO because I was a good Catholic girl, and then went on to lead a fruitful and spotless life. But you know that didn't happen because if it did, you wouldn't be reading this book. But I can't that…I didn't' say NO. I'm not even sure I entertained second thoughts; I had too many bills and no prospects to pay them. So, again back to the TV show, we cut to a scene where I'm accompanying Michelle into the dingy strip club where she danced. The rest, as they say, is history.

We'll get back to my first experiences as a stripper, but at this point, I wanted to set the stage by giving you all a little 101 tutorial on the sex industry in Honolulu. I will only briefly mention prostitutes because they are not part of my story even though they are a significant component of the sex trade in Honolulu. You can see "Ladies of the Evening" parading in their finest seductive outfits every night on Kalakaua and Kuhio Avenues, the two main roads through Waikiki, sometimes walking right in front of the Waikiki police station. Appearance-wise they run the gamut from beautiful to those that leave you wondering if they ever have any customers at all. All lead sad and risky lives of pimps, disease, arrests, and the possibility of being beaten up or killed by customers. Seeing them, especially the more attractive ones, makes me angry. I want to walk up to them and say "Get off the street, there's better ways to make a living with your body by dancing or being a hostess"; better money with less danger. The prostitutes aside, there are a number of other options in the Honolulu nighttime sex industry for lonely men, single or married with a wandering eye; and there is a discernible hierarchy in these options. If we were going to discuss prostitutes, I would have them on the bottom of this hierarchy labeled "Last Resort." A little higher up on the food chain are the massage parlors featuring "the company of lovely young ladies" according to the newspaper ads. I know what they offer for money over and above the massages wink wink…and so does everyone else including the police, so I often wonder why they aren't busted on a weekly basis. But for some reason they aren't and life continues on unimpeded in Honolulu society with no Wrath of God consequences, much to the consternation of our church going brethren. Maybe the police feel the massage parlors actually serve a social purpose of keeping would be perverts off the streets by providing a willing and convenient sexual outlet for urges they would otherwise try to satisfy by molesting or raping unwilling women. Again, I often wonder if our morality laws are doing a great disservice to the American society at large. Although I don't agree with street hookers, what's wrong with a legal sexual service? It's an accepted business in other countries and they don't seem worse off for allowing it. A lot of countries have legal brothels. I'm just not sure I see the harm in having the same in the U.S. If they're legal and managed, it means a safer and healthier experience (less sexual diseases or violence) for all concerned. This is not to say I'm in favor of human trafficking where unwilling girls are forced into prostitution, but what is the harm of a woman participating in the world's oldest profession by choice? Just a thought...but enough me standing on my soapbox. My opinion is my opinion, and I don't think I'm going to be able to make even the slightest dent in this country's laws written by morally frigid, sexually repressed, religious assholes. The only sexual misadventures our country's leadership permits are those they can personally get away with in private with remorse and a sense of moral commitment being expressed only after they get caught. You know, I would pay all of the money I have in this world just to see one of our slimy politicians actually admit to, or brag about his sexual conquests. For example: "President Clinton, did you have sex with Monica

Lewinsky"? His (my recommended response): "Hell yes, so what? She was willing, I was willing. Why Not? Have you seen my wife?"

The second tier of the Hawaii sex industry is the hostess bars, an artifact of the Asian influence in Hawaii. Most are small Korean-owned establishments consisting of a small bar area, a few booths or tables, and a Karaoke machine. They advertise their services in the newspaper with catchy names such as "Club Meet Me", "Club By Me", "Club VIP" and not willing to miss out on a high profile event, "Club Y2K." They also switch ownership quite often, with a number of new clubs being advertised weekly as "Grand Opening Opening Under New Management." They are called hostess bars because they employ a number of women (actually they're advertised as girls, I guess to make them seem younger), or hostesses, who will gladly sit down and talk to lonely customers for the short duration of a $20 Lady's drink. I think the word "employ" is a little misleading. Although the girls are considered as employees, the bar actually pays them little or nothing. They are more like independent contractors who make their money by enticing customers to buy them these Lady's drinks and then sharing the profit from the drink 50/50 with the bar (the woman gets $10 and the bar $10). The number of drinks purchased and the frequency of their purchase is entirely between the girl and her customer.

Hostesses may also make illegal separate arrangements to meet customers after work hours for further adventures. Although some of these out-of-the-club liaisons may be legitimate dates, most are more sexually focused with an exchange of money a precursor for this date. I know, I know, I just described prostitution and I said I wouldn't. I like to think this assignation for sexual purposes is different than a "john" making an arrangement with a streetwalker on a street corner, although it's a very subtle difference. A hostess bar arrangement is more along the nature of a date, just with compensated sex as an understood component of the date. Both partners know each other, the guy probably having come into the club several times previously and developed a sort of a relationship with a girl before asking her out. And the sex? Not sure how you can call it illegal when sex seems to be an expected component of any legitimate date where the girl is expected to put out because her date bought her dinner and a little entertainment like a movie? One of the attractions of hostess bars is a customer can have his choice of girls in a variety of nationalities depending on what he likes - Korean, Japanese, Filipino, Vietnamese, etc. You notice I didn't say Caucasian, there just doesn't seem to be any white girls working in Hostess bars for some reason. I've never figured that out. Maybe it's because Hostess Bars are an ingrained part of Asian culture and their customers prefer Asian girls. After all, we are superior in knowing how to take care of a man! Ha Ha. Some of the hostesses are young, but there are a lot of older women who have no marketable job skills other than being a hostess. Most are looking to find a husband or a steady boyfriend. You will never hear me say anything bad about hostess bars. I believe they serve a significant societal purpose in bringing a little companionship to a lonely male population in Hawaii. I'm actually surprised hostess bars are not more prevalent in the mainland U.S. other than those cities with a large Asian population such as Los Angeles. I'd like to think Hostess Bars cut down on the number of rapes and divorces in Hawaii because they offer the one thing (other than sex) that guys often seek, single or married – companionship with a willing female. For the price of a Lady's drink, the girls are very good listeners for a guy to pour out his problems or have a few minutes of non-judgmental female company. The girls may not understand everything a customer says because of language difficulties, but they are well trained to act like they do and provide the correct soothing responses at the appropriate moments. It's obviously a sympathetic response these men aren't getting from their wives or girlfriends. Believe me, Asian girls are good at this sort of thing, I prove it every night, even for the most obnoxious customers. I've thought about being a hostess from time to time when I get tired of getting naked but I don't think I'd have the patience or willingness to "entertain" a customer by sitting with him for an extended period of time, especially if he's trying to constantly cop a feel. Also, the money I make as a stripper is several times better than what a hostess makes even on her best days.

Finally, to finish this dissertation on the Honolulu sex trade, let's talk about the Exotic (nude) dancing clubs; the strip clubs. They basically come in three varieties, high class, middle class and low class; each class being determined by the quality of the club facilities and the youth and beauty of the dancers. Although I will go into more detail later, here is a quick reference of what you'll find in each of these club types:

High class clubs – The clubs are first rate when it comes to amenities and you won't be disappointed in the quality of the dancers, all young and beautiful…not the worn out strippers lesser clubs feature. Some are from the mainland and just passing through to make good money while they enjoy Hawaii. These girls are like professional athletes rotating from club to club depending on the money being offered and their sense of adventure and travel. So you're living in Minnesota and want to get away for the winter? Go to Hawaii, spend a few months out of the cold taking your clothes off and make a lot of money doing it. Some even have agents (or boyfriends along for the ride) who negotiate for them. High class clubs on the mainland are often called Gentlemen's Clubs to make them seem classier but whether you're in Hawaii or the mainland you'll pay a lot of money for the privilege of being in the company of their dancers both in the cost of frequently "feeding the garter belt" and buying lady's drinks.

Middle and lower class clubs - local girls, not quite so good looking or young. More than a few girls in the low class clubs are well past their prime and hanging on to the life for some reason. They may have danced in a high class club earlier in life but could never make that transition from dancing to a more normal job or life, i.e. they had no Plan B or their Plan B failed and they had no

Plan C. Many of the girls in the lower class clubs just never had the good looks desired by the higher class club and were stuck with making due in lesser venues. For some, this is their first job in America being as one reviewer of Hawaii strip clubs described it in an article I saw on the Internet, just "off the boat", meaning they are new émigrés with little education and English. I guess you get what you pay for. I feel compelled; however, to defend each and every one of them, after all what are their alternatives? Stripping and hostessing are pretty much the only jobs they can make enough money to live on, especially if their English isn't good - three to four times the money they would make in minimum wage jobs. And believe me, none of them intend these jobs to be lifelong careers; they all have plans to meet and marry a rich customer who will take them out of the sex trade life. It happens just enough to keep them all optimistic, after all there are a lot of horny, lonely guys out there, and these girls meet them every night at work…and they are so eager to please... what man can resist? Although I don't really differentiate between the middle and lower class clubs, there are differences, the most telling of which is that in the lower class clubs you are two or three Lady's drink away from a small negotiation and a hand job in the club or an after-hours adventure in the nearest cheap hotel. These lower class strip clubs and the hostess bars I described earlier are the most prone to be raided by the police or liquor commission. Don't ask me why, other than they are a little looser with sexual favors than the higher end clubs. But, again, my perverse nature says clubs like these get raided because they are a little late with their payment to the police or liquor commission welfare funds. This is just my opinion, so don't go pointing fingers shouting corruption, but it's a popular sentiment in the hostess community. Also, if they raid the higher class clubs they might accidentally catch a city or state politician with his face two inches from the crotch of a naked dancer. Every so often you will see a news broadcast or read in the newspaper about such and such a hostess club being raided with pictures of handcuffed girls being put into police cars. The tragedy is not so much for the owners of these establishments, they'll pay their fines, vow to be more forthcoming in the future with contributions to the above mentioned welfare funds, and then open their clubs back up as if nothing happened; it's the girls that suffer. They're often not U.S. citizens and arrests for prostitution can (and frequently do) mean deportation for them. This not only affects the girls, if affects the families they were sending money to back in their home countries.

Anyway, given the definition of the clubs I just provided, let's get back to the story. The club my friend Michelle talked me into dancing for was definitely not high class. I was shocked to say the least when I walked through the front door. Dark, dirty, and sleazy are somehow not strong enough adjectives to express my first impression of what I saw. The smell also assaulted my senses. A heady mixture of cigarette smoke (you could still smoke in the clubs when I first started to strip), stale beer, and a sperm-infused carpet. It was an odor that would cling to your hair and clothes hours after you left the club, forcing you to take a long hot shower as the first order of business when you got home. I would have taken a shower anyway just to try and wash the sleaze away. The club featured two long stages with chairs along all sides for men who wanted a really up close and personal view of the dancers (for tips of course). There were two rows of booths between the stages and a number of other booths along the walls surrounding the stage area. Some of the booths were well lit and out in the open, others were located in darker corners; I would find out later what these booths were for. The club also had several smaller rooms upstairs for more intimate one-on-one dancing and personal contact, i.e. the customers got to feel the girls up and get a lap dance while doing it, again for a price the girl and club shared equally. This was definitely not the "Gentlemen's Club" you see advertised on the mainland where there is at least a pretense of class and oh, by the way, dancing girls for your amusement and entertainment. This club had no such pretentions. It was there for sexual amusement and gratification…period.

The customers had three goals in mind – get drunk, look at pussy, and get a feel and the girls seem glad to help these customers achieve these goals if it meant more money for them. So here I was, a sheltered girl fresh out of a small, rural Filipino province walking into an environment like this. And did I mention I was only 20, still underage? For a couple of seconds, I just stood there with my mouth open, wondering what the hell I was getting myself into. I wasn't a virgin by any stretch of imagination, remember I used to be married, but the sheer open sexuality of this club was very intimidating at first glance. Michelle; however, had little patience for my timidity, she wanted to get onstage and start making money. So, just as I was about ready to turn around and walk out of the club, Michelle grabbed my hand and introduced me to the club manager. He was suspicious at first and asked for my ID since I needed to be 21 to work in the club. As I said, I was only 20, so I thought this job was going to end before it started. Michelle, not to be put off, told the manager I had forgotten my ID at home, but not to worry, I was over 21. The manager reluctantly agreed, I think in large part because he was short of girls that night and as I said, I'm not an ugly girl. So I was hired. I know you're probably thinking I was very hesitant to take my clothes off in front of total strangers and the first time was probably a traumatic experience for me. It might have been but for Michelle who took the situation in hand and told me in no uncertain terms to watch her and do what she did. And I did...... and never looked back. I've been asked a few times what this first experience was like. In fact, the friend I have helping me write my story was a little insistent on me expanding on this as a point of interest for this book. I think everyone wonders how they would feel getting naked for strangers. It may not be difficult for men because I think they're natural exhibitionists and like waggling their weenies around, especially if the women they're stripping for are pawing at them and offering sex. In fact that might be a man's version of paradise. Women on the other hand, are a little more reluctant, especially if they were sheltered growing up. I have to admit I did feel a few qualms, after all I was a good Catholic girl (well, kinda good) coming from a very strict upbringing. So, if it makes you feel better, looking back, I have to say there were a few seconds of hesitation but not much more. I've always been a "do whatever it takes to get the job done" type of a person. It also helped that my first customer was young and good looking, not someone old and lecherous, and he had a fist full of money he was practically panting to give to me. So off came my clothes as fast as he could put money in my garter - so much for traumatic. I actually only danced for him just a few minutes, enough for him to get a look under my panties before he moved on to another dancer, but it was an experience that launched me on my way to being a professional stripper. If you want to know the truth, it was actually a little liberating. I could actually feel the power I had over my customers, to tease and please at will; more importantly, I learned how easy it was to coax money out of them when lust was clogging their brain synapses. As the night progressed, I got very much into the swing of things helped by all of the money I was making, and when the club closed I had almost $600 in hand. I was amazed....and hooked.

I got my first bitter experience; however, about my fifth night of dancing. By then, I was feeling comfortable stripping and interacting with customers but then came a customer who asked me for a private dance upstairs. This would be my first time there but I didn't think I'd have a problem handling it. He contracted me to dance five songs for him at $35 a song. Usually, these songs could be paid for ahead of time at the bar or separately with the dancer who would then later reimburse the bar. I chose the latter and allowed him to watch me move around naked on a small private stage while he masturbated and felt me up. At the end of the five songs, he ejaculated, stood up and walked out of the room not bothering to pay me. I was stunned at first and when I went running after him out of the room he was already gone. He got a free good time but I was the one that got screwed. Lesson learned? After that, it was always money up front before I did anything....period. $35 x 5 = $175, a really expensive lesson, but one that has served me well over the years...bottom line, never believe or trust customers. With the help of that lesson, I was a seasoned pro within a month, making more money than I ever thought possible and achieving the independence I had been looking for since I turned 18. Don't get me wrong though, it wasn't an uneventful yellow brick road to success, there were a couple of big bumps - the last one ending my employment in this club and my life as a dancer for a couple of years. First, for some reason, I guess my small size, I had attracted the hostile intentions of one of the dancers, a local girl (read Hawaiian or Samoan). I can't recall ever saying anything bad or insulting to her, just minding my own business dancing, but one night she assaulted me in the lady's bathroom. She was much bigger than me so it was no contest. She wrestled me to the ground and began to beat my face with her fists breaking the left side of my jaw. She was immediately fired, of course, but for months afterward, I was constantly looking out for her whenever I left the club after work. I was also on the lookout for some of her friends in the club. Although nothing further happened and I was back at work the next week, it made me wary of any relationship with my fellow dancers, a precaution I still follow today. Believe it or not, this same thing happened years later in the Hot Zone when another fellow dancer took a severe disliking to me. She was a big local girl with a lot of tattoos like the first girl. Not a raging beauty so I think she rationalized she wasn't getting any business because I was stealing her clients. Happily, this incident didn't result in me getting my ass kicked again but there were a lot of threats and tension. Like the first incident, it just pointed out the need to be alert for trouble from both customers and my fellow dancers; after all I'm only 4'11'' so pretty much everyone physically outmatches me.

As I said, I had two unpleasant incidents in this first club. The second was being arrested for prostitution in 2002. ARRESTED….ME!!! Get your mind out of the gutter, I wasn't having sex in one of the back rooms of the club and I didn't take a well-paying customer home. I was only giving a lap dance and allowing the customer a little feel, business as usual; something I had to do to stay competitive with the other dancers. BUT, it turns out this customer was a Honolulu vice cop. Damn! For clarification, the charge of prostitution in Hawaii covers a lot of possibilities; just letting a customer touch you inappropriately anywhere on your body can result in a prostitution charge.

Likewise, it is also illegal for a dancer to touch a customer or to even touch herself. Generally, if this type of activity is detected by Liquor Commission agents, both the offending girl and the club get fined, with the girl probably being fired by the club afterwards to add insult to injury. If you're nabbed by a vice copy…you get arrested…period. Lower class clubs, such as the one I was working in, can acquire a reputation for this kind of activity despite the illegalities. It's kind of a chicken and egg situation. The customers come in expecting a little latitude from the girls on what exactly is appropriate behavior. If the girls aren't willing to bend the rules just a little, customers will migrate to those that do. The bar owners know this and I think secretly encouraged a little raunchier behavior from their girls, better for business. The State Liquor Commission and the vice cops also know this and I'm firmly convinced their agents get a little "something – something" from the club owners not to make raids. Again, legal disclaimer….this is just an opinion from criminal me, but it's one based on my observations. Well this time, either the money wasn't enough or they had to make a quota of arrests to justify their job. Enter the stupid new girl - ME. Needless to say, I was arrested, along with a number of other girls in the club for just being in the club. I say I was arrested, but it was pretty subtle, I wasn't led out of the club in handcuffs or anything. In fact, I didn't even find out I had been arrested until several weeks later when I got a summons in the mail to show up in court at such and such time. Maybe I was fortunate to get busted by a vice cop instead of the liquor commission because I didn't get fined, nor did the club; I just got arrested. Talk about putting a positive spin on "just getting arrested." To the other girls in the club, this was an expected consequence of their job....old hat that they took very calmly. They advised me to hire the same lawyer they did, someone they had used successfully before. I don't really recall why, but for some reason, I hired my own lawyer who advised me to plead "No Contest" to the charge of prostitution. My whole motivation at the time was just to get this thing over with as quickly as possible, so I submitted a "No Contest" plea, paid a $500 fine, and was given two years probation. The other girls who used a different lawyer? Their case was dismissed. So now I was a criminal with a criminal record and not for something neat like assault and battery...but for prostitution.

This whole incident scared the shit out of me and I quit dancing. I think you've all heard of a TV show called scared straight where they have a bunch of convicts come in and tell juvenile delinquents how bad life is in jail. Well, I was definitely scared straight. I found another job, a normal job working as desk clerk in one of the larger hotels in downtown Honolulu, just a block from Waikiki beach. I also made my first foray into entrepreneurship by opening a small dress shop. I'll tell you more about these jobs later when I discuss my continuing efforts to get out of stripping. But back to the situation at hand, my ARREST haunted me for years. In 2003, a year after I had been arrested, I flew back to the Philippines on vacation. When I tried to re-enter the United States, I almost couldn't. The airports still had very stringent security 9-11 security measures in place and when the Immigration officials saw me trying to enter the country with a criminal record for prostitution I was detained in the airport while they decided what to do with me even though I had a green card. Seeing there was a problem and my whole future going down the drain, I called an immigration lawyer, I had hired before I left for the Philippines to work my citizenship, for help. She came down and told Immigration to either send me back to the Philippines (thanks) or let me go. Fortunately, they opted for the latter and let me re-enter the country, but right up until time I started writing this book, I have been too scared to see my family in the Philippines again fearing a repeat of the incident. One further kicker in this whole episode is something I just found out just a few weeks ago and it really pisses me off. I recently hired a new immigration lawyer to help me make yet another attempt at becoming a U.S. citizen. My first lawyer was basically worthless and I could see she wasn't really making any effort to help me. As part of the work up for my case, the new lawyer asked me to get a copy of my arrest record. Up until then, I had only a single piece of paper saying I had been charged and put on probation. When I looked at my arrest record, it indicated my prostitution charge had been dismissed two weeks after my court date. I was floored and pissed again. THOSE BASTARDS! I had been kept dancing on a string from 2002 until now thinking I was still under a cloud from this arrest and as a consequence was too afraid to visit my family; in essence I was a prisoner in my adopted country. I was never notified of this change in status of my case by anyone, the court officials or my old lawyer, anyone! I think that was wrong and totally inconsiderate. When I told the friend helping me write this book about this arrest and me being afraid all these years he started laughing. Not about the arrest but about the fact of not knowing all these years the case had been dismissed. He's a BASTARD too…but he knows that and is even proud of the fact. This is the same friend; the one I told you can make me cry…Cocksucker!!

One last entry for my arrest incident that just occurred as I was updating this book – I got my arrest purged from my record. It wasn't hard. It just took a little money and some patience but it all paid off so now I'm free and clear of all legal impediments. Woo Hoo and the road is now clear for me to finally become a U.S. citizen.

I Don't Want to Strip Anymore

By now you've probably guessed I've grown disillusioned with my life as a stripper over the years; my attempts to escape have been many and varied. None have been successful, although they did allow me to quit dancing for varying amounts of time and reassess my life. Marrying my second husband was a first attempt...well sort of, since I did continue to work while we were married, just not as often. I also tried working in a number of hotels in Waikiki, was a car salesman....TWICE, and opened and failed at three businesses. Some would argue being a car salesman was not really an escape from a sleazy job, in fact being a stripper might be more respectable. As a stripper you only take your clothes off for a customer. Car salesmen try to screw them. Ha Ha. I would laugh, but I was both a stripper and a car salesman at the same time, so what does that say about me. St. Peter is going to have a field day with me when I see him at the Pearly Gates. I think if there is such a thing as karma and reincarnation, I'm really screwed. With my bad karma, I'll probably reincarnate as a virus or an STD. Ha Ha. Anyway, back on topic, we'll go back to talking about stripping in a minute, this time in my current club, the Hot Zone, but if you don't mind, I'd like to first give you a little more details on my attempts to stop stripping. I hope it will give you more perspective about what I think of my stripping life. You can make a lot of money stripping but it comes at the expense of your self-esteem and your pride. The longer I dance and the older I get, the more uneasy I feel about what I'm doing and the direction…or lack of direction, my life is going. This internal damage makes me try all of the harder to get out of the life and find a profession I can be proud of…you know, get a respectable career that I can pursue until I'm old and wrinkled. I also worry about my shelf life as a stripper which is usually only a few years; stripping can age you physically and mentally very quickly. My nightmare is to wake up one day and find myself as one of those sad strippers you see in every club still hanging on even though no one wants to see them naked anymore.

- *Would you like to buy a dress?*

Perfect Fashion. That was the name of the dress store I started up with a friend while I was dancing in my first exotic night club. Even though I was making good money dancing, I could see even then at my young age, stripping was not a job I wanted as a life-long profession. As with all of my later self-employment attempts, I started out with great hopes and failed, with both my hopes and money going down the drain. We began by selling dresses out of my garage and then progressed to renting a small store. We built up a large inventory of what I thought were good looking dresses from both purchasing on line and through several trips to distributors in California. The dresses were smart and up-to-date with current styles which reflected in good sales. However….and here is the however that has always plagued my attempts at owning a business, both my partner and myself soon found we didn't have sufficient time to open and manage the store. We both had other jobs that were also placing demands on our time. Myself, I was still making a lot of money dancing so I think my enthusiasm in keeping a business open that didn't make as much money and in fact resulted in me losing money because it kept me from dancing when I ran the store dwindled. I have to admit there was also a large measure of laziness thrown in…hey, we were young and stupid. Damn…I keep saying that…is young and stupid a disease? We absolutely had to fit nightclubbing all night into our schedules which made it hard to get up in the morning and open the shop. So…as I said, we failed. It wouldn't be my only business failure and money pit, I had more in my future.

- Would you like a room?

After I divorced Husband #2, I found myself struggling to make a living doing a normal job. I no longer danced (remember me quitting my first dancing job after I got arrested?) and I was determined to keep it that way so I worked as a night desk clerk in a large hotel just off of the Waikiki strip. The pay was nowhere near what I earned in the club but I enjoyed the job and I was good at what I did; I keep telling you I'm not dumb. Besides managing the front deck, I also kept the books as a night time auditor. I got to meet a lot of interesting people, most were great customers, excited in be in Hawaii and very friendly to the hotel staff. Some were complete assholes, unforgiving of any breach of protocol or imagined slight to their dignity. I'm not sure why they even bothered to come to Hawaii, not a cheap trip by any means, if they were going to spend their entire vacation being unhappy. I'm not saying we were screwed up as a hotel staff, we weren't. We were total professionals with the customer's best interests in heart. I got along great with my co-workers and managers and I worked my butt off to not only be the best at my job, but also to succeed in the tourism business. And I was committed; I got two Associates Degrees during this time, one in Tourism and Hotel Management and another in Business. The problem? The Hotel unions. Even though I was qualified to move into a better job or even into management by both training and experience, I wasn't allowed to do so because of longevity, I was still junior as far time in the company. Employees with more longevity were given the first opportunities for advancement even if they were total idiots. Let me pontificate a little more on unions. I'm probably going to get into trouble here, but what the hell, I've already insulted the Catholic church and Hawaii law enforcement, so why not Unions. Maybe I've also insulted God since both the Catholic Church and unions seem to feel they have a special relationship with the Big Guy. To be straight up, I hate unions. I feel they protect the incompetent at the expense of those who are better qualified, want to excel, and would make better managers in the long run. Longevity is not, and should not be, a major qualification for advancement. That is why businesses are failing all over the world now; they're run by idiots who have outlasted or out lived their peers. I make this statement being fully aware of how unions got started and the excellent work they did protecting workers against truly abysmal working conditions and unfair labor practices in the late nineteenth century. I get it. But I think they've outlived their usefulness because there are not strong laws to protect worker's rights. Now, unions are just a major impediment to the ability of a business being able to make a profit or even survive. Take the U.S. auto industry for example, where workers make huge hourly wages and enjoy great benefits all negotiated by their union using the leverage of crippling strikes if management didn't go along with their demands. This is great for the workers until they get laid off because the American car industry can no longer compete with foreign auto makers who can build cheaper cars with no unions to contend with.   And what do the Unions do?   Work with management to help salvage the business, maybe with wage concessions or some roll back of the benefits? NO…in fact they demand even more.   The result?   The unemployment lines get longer. But back to my story. After a while, I got disenchanted at the glass ceiling keeping me from advancing in a profession I really liked. I was also starting to feel the pinch of an income that was much less than what I was making stripping. My whole goal since I turned 18 was being independent and staying away from my mother and I could see that without a husband to help support me, my small hotel paycheck had me spiraling back into living with her, something I really didn't want. As a consequence, I was forced back into the warm embrace of the stripping life, this time in my current club, the Hot Zone. This wasn't the end of my attempts to stop stripping by any means to the consternation of the club owner.   In fact my stints of dancing in the Hot Zone have been interspersed with frequent escape attempts I think you should know about. After all, they're part of my life.

- *Would you like to buy some vegetables?*

In late 2007, I rented a small stall in Honolulu's Chinatown to sell vegetables and Filipino food items. I invested all of the money I had saved up from dancing to rent the space, furnish it, and buy initial inventory. I hired my Mom to help run it because I needed to keep dancing to keep the money flowing as we tried to get the store up and running. As with any new store, I expected it would take time to build up enough of a clientele base to make the store profitable, and I was prepared to keep dancing to give it that time. On the plus side, the experience I gained opening a store from scratch was invaluable and will serve me well in any future business endeavor. I learned how to negotiate rent, buy goods from vendors, arrange these goods for sale, set up my cash register and EBT outlet for customer to pay me, and take care of the hundreds of other small details small business owners face every day. The downside? I lost my financial ass. Here's where having a little business experience before I began this adventure would have helped greatly. The stall I rented was way too small to sell enough goods to make a living no matter how hard I tried. It was also situated in a bad place on the larger market floor because every customer I saw had already purchased their vegetables, the same vegetables I was selling, at other stalls closer to the front door. With more experience, I would have been able to see this stall was a disaster in the making and had no upside. The previous owner had failed, as had the owner preceding him. It could have been worse, I guess. Again in my innocence, I had signed a three-year lease for the stall. Other owners told me later I could have rented it for a six month trial period. Duh on me! Being held to the three-year lease would have forced me into bankruptcy by requiring me to continue paying for the stall even though I couldn't afford to keep it stocked with merchandise to sell. So I wrote a very professional letter to the agency that managed the market explaining politely I needed to back out of the rental lease or I would have to declare bankruptcy. Although they had me over a legal barrel, for some reason they let me go. I had a short interview with the agency manager right after I submitted the letter. He said he had watched me closely because he knew the history of the stall and had seen how hard I tried to make the store a success. He said he would let me out of the lease if I could get someone else to take it over. Amazingly, someone wanted it right away. They also failed very quickly thereafter, not even getting to the point of displaying goods. I don't regret this experience even though I lost all of my savings; it was a real life education you can't get in school. My lessons learned? Investigate, prepare, advertise, work hard, and be prepared to fail. I think it's the "being prepared to fail" that prevents most people from wanting to start their own business. This job is a significant bullet in my resume if you need to hire someone with business experience. I certainly know intimately many of the pitfalls that cause businesses to fail.

- Need a new or used car?

Go ahead and make the joke that I took a step down on the social acceptability ladder from being a stripper to taking a job as a car salesman.......TWICE...Ha Ha, very funny. Yes, I had two separate jobs selling cars – Nissans and Chevrolets. Each of these forays into the auto profession was a year apart. In other words, I tried to sell cars, quit, and then a year later tried again. In a way, there is a relationship between stripping and selling cars other than the requirement to have low morals and no conscience. In both occupations, you try to talk customers out of their hard earned money. Ha Ha. (These are jokes people) Maybe it's the competitive juices in me, I actually liked selling cars but trying to live on sales commissions is not for the weak, especially during a down economy. It's also definitely not considered a traditional woman's career. I had only one other fellow female co-worker. My main competitors were a mix of young guys and old veterans who probably sold Fred Flintstone his first car. I don't use the term competitor lightly. They <u>were all sharks</u> and as the newbie I was literally thrown to the sharks. Although we were classified as a sales team, the reality was we were a collection of highly motivated (and predatory) individuals stalking the car lot looking for customers. Whenever someone drove or walked onto the lot, the first one to see him or her raised their hand and yelled "Up", and then charged off with a big smile to greet the customer and not let them leave until they bought something. I'm pretty sure tackling them as they walked off the lot without buying a car would not have been permitted legally, but I don't think the dealership management would have balked at such tactics. I admit I was at a distinct disadvantage when I was first hired. I didn't know anything about cars other than where the steering wheel was and what hole to put the gasoline in. I had to learn quickly and to my credit I did, or I didn't hesitate to ask for help. To their credit, my fellow salesmen (the guys) were never slow in helping me if I had a question, in that sense, I guess we were a team. I did have a couple of significant advantages over the guys however. First, as I said before, I'm hot looking with great boobs. A lot of men would come in just to look and end up buying a car just to impress me. Again, like the club, I had a no dating the customers rule but that didn't stop them from trying, probably because I would conveniently forget to tell them about my no dating policy until after they bought the car Ha Ha. Also, I <u>was</u> still dancing at the time and I passed out business cards to all of the customers I danced for. My teammates were always puzzled whenever a guy would come in asking for me. Ha Ha. Do I feel guilty? Hell, NO! In the car business, you use every advantage you have to gain a competitive edge. You need to if you want to survive. I know a million ways to emphasize the fact I have great boobs…Ha Ha. Since I was having moderate success based on my advantages, I was able to be magnanimous with the other salesmen on certain occasions. Often, I would be the first one to see a customer come in and would yell "Up", then give another of the salesmen a chance to make a sale because I had already made my quota of sales that week courtesy of my other customer resources. I'm not all about the money despite what I say later in the book about my stripping business plan, i.e. get everything you can from the customer.

I do have to say I saw a lot of things in the car dealership business that even rubbed my morality the wrong way. I guess every business has its skeletons. One thing that particularly bothered me was how we took advantage of the customers when it came to their trade-ins. We would pay as little as possible for a customer's car and then turn it around for a great profit. Some may say that's the American way of doing business, buy low and sell high, but I couldn't justify cheating a customer out of his hard earned money. I struck back on more than one occasion, one of which comes to mind. An old lady, a widow whose husband had just died, came in to buy a smaller car using her husband's large car as a trade in. The dealership was going to cheat her and I couldn't see adding to her misfortunes so I pulled her to the side and said I'd sell it for her outside the dealership and then split the profit with her. I guess it was my honest face, or she was also thinking the dealership was trying to screw her, so she said yes. I could have been fired on the spot for doing this, but I sold the car for $3000 and gave her half, much better than the $300 the dealership was offering. I had a friend for life and now that I've admitted this indiscretion in writing, I'll probably be blacklisted from ever selling cars again. It's not that other salesmen don't do the same thing to survive, they just don't admit it in a book.

My demise from the car business wasn't that I couldn't hack the long hours or the stress of having to make sales, I could and I was good at it. I enjoyed the interactions with the customers and the give and take of selling. And I liked the camaraderie of working – competing – with my fellow salesmen. They were like brothers when business was slow, never pulling punches when they were joking with me; but beware when the sales game was afoot...like I said they were sharks, well so was I. What finally caused me to quit was my feet I got plantar fasciitis in both heels from being on my feet all day in shoes that were only meant to look good while walking short distances. It got bad it was agonizing to even touch my feet. I had no choice but to quit and go back to dancing full time where the only thing I would hurt was my knees and my pride...CRAP.

Damn it! Back to being a Stripper – The Hot Zone

Now that we've returned from the intermission where I described my efforts to lead a normal life, let's get back to the point of the story - my stripping experiences. After all, I think that's what you bought this book for. Ha Ha. This time the setting is my current club, the Hot Zone, a significant step up in class and in fact, probably the premier club in Hawaii. No, it's not a real club....well, it is a real club, I just changed the name so I wouldn't get my ass sued off....and I have such a nice ass...Ha Ha. I could tell from the moment I entered the Hot Zone on my first day of work it was miles above my previous club in class and money making potential. It was less dingy and had prettier dancers. It also lacked the pervasive sperm-infused, spilled beer carpet bouquet that still dominates memories of my first club. Most importantly, the club had Conduct Rules it enforced vigorously, including a "No Touching" rule. The club drew in a better class of customer with more money and a willingness to spend it. Don't get me wrong, we're not talking about all millionaires here, just a good mix of working class and customers that could legitimately be called millionaires, all willing to feed the "garter." Just the place for an enterprising entrepreneur like myself.

Let me play tour guide for a minute and give you a short description of what the club looks like. Walking in from the parking lot in the back of the club, you will see four stages in a row, A, B, C, D, and a fifth stage, E, placed off to the right side of the club. They're not the elaborate glass stages you may see in mainland "Gentlemen's Clubs" with production quality light shows. Instead they're well used plain wood-framed stages with tile-covered floors scarred over the years by the stiletto heels of the dancers they support. Each stage can comfortably accommodate four girls, but I've seen as many as eight when the club is really busy and all the dancers want to be on stage making money. Although each stage has a traditional stripper pole at each corner, the dancers don't use them much, preferring to kneel in front of customers sitting on chairs next to the stage. This allows for a close one-on-one interaction that lets the dancers talk intimately to their customers while slowly and seductively disrobing and posing. Because they're on their knees a lot, each girl uses a small personal pad to kneel on when she's performing. You'd be amazed how hard the floor of the stage gets if you're on your knees for any length of time; I have lots of bruises to prove that. The pads also serve as repository for the dollar bills customers stick in the dancer's garters to encourage their scandalous behavior. Ha Ha. Although there are no mandatory stage assignments, the dancers tend to habitually limit their dancing to only one or two stages. I don't know why but I do the same thing, pretty much dancing only on Stage E where the other Asian girls dance. It's probably a mutual support thing, dancing naked in front of strangers is very uncomfortable, but it's a little easier if you're dancing alongside friends who speak your same language. This clustering of dancers also makes it easier for customers to walk into a club and know exactly where their favorite dancers are. I also like Stage E because it allows me to work with more than one customer at a time. If I see a favorite customer come in while I'm dancing for someone else, I'll have a waiter conduct him to a booth on the other side of the club with a promise I'll get with him as soon as I can. This is much more preferable to having the arriving customer sitting close by and getting jealous watching me be sweet to my current customer to get money out of him. I'll give you a little more details on how I treat a customer later, but needless to say my interactions with one customer is not for another of my customers to ogle. Juggling two is about my limit; I've seen other dancers juggle three or more routinely and not have their customers at each other's throats. It takes a lot of sweet talking to pull that off.

As you enter the Hot Zone, you're immediately assaulted by loud music, mostly current tunes of the day. I don't think I've ever been in a strip club that doesn't play music several decibels above the pain threshold for human ears. My first club had huge speakers placed all around the club – both in the ceiling and on the floor next to the stages. To my mind, the right kind of music can be a scene setter for the girls, a background for them to apply their own particular dancing styles against. I'm probably in the minority here and other dancers have their own opinions, but I've always thought slow, sensual music puts customers into a receptive mood for spending money on the dancers. You see, a key to our success is building an intimate bond with a customer within the first few minutes of them sitting down in front of us; kind of like speed dating. We want them to have this feeling of shared intimacy. We want them to fall in love with us while we're taking our clothes off. Love really opens their wallets and turns off their brains, well at least their big brains Ha Ha. So how do I establish this intimacy? Easy, I talk to them like they're the most interesting person in my life, and for that particular moment in time, they are since they have the money. Ha Ha. A lot of customers have probably never had a girl actually seem interested in what they have to say or even want to talk to them for that matter. I ask about their families, their job, their hobbies, etc. I don't give them a "holier than thou face" if I find out they're married. In fact a lot of them like to brag about their wives and show me their pictures. So despite me wondering why they're even in a strip club in the first place, I just smile and comment about how their wife must be a wonderful person [who doesn't know you're here]. I'm very good at giving the impression that whatever a customer says is the funniest or most interesting thing I've heard all day. I try to give them a real girlfriend experience (GFE for all you punters), getting as physically close to them as I can - within the limits of the no touching laws of course. We'll talk more about that later. I have to admit, I do break the law every once in a while to help foster the feeling of intimacy. No, it's not what you're thinking, get your mind out of the gutter. I'll caress his arms, hold hands with him, blow in his ear, and talk to him in a low, intimate voice. I'll hang my head out over the edge of the stage and drape my hair over his head and body. I will even sit backwards on the stage and lean back into him, forcing him to put his arms around me. OOOOO LA LA. It works 99% of the time and the dollars flow out of his wallet. How can any red-blooded male resist holding a naked or nearly naked healthy young female in his arms? Lust is a wonderful thing. Remember what I said earlier about trying to keep my customers separated in different parts of the club to cut down on jealousy? This is why. And, for the record for you law enforcement types, WHAT IS THE HARM? My customer gets a memorable experience, a little loneliness assuaged, and I make a few dollars from him. NO HARM, NO SEX, NO FOUL, right? I know that everything I do is all an act and the customer does too (at least I hope he does), but so what? Call it a cheap therapy session. It certainly would be more expensive for him to actually see a professional therapist to talk about his problems and they probably won't get naked at anytime during the session like I do. In fact, I'm not sure you would want to see them naked...Ha Ha. So...the bottom line is...we both walk away from the encounter happier, him probably much happier then when he walked into the club. I've had great success with the way I treat my customers. I once danced for a single customer for more than three hours all the while yanking my garter out at a frequent pace for him to fill with dollar bills. My goal is to not let a customer get tired of me or get bored….and to make sure he doesn't leave while he still has money to spend. Ha Ha. For the three hour dance, although the money was great, and the customer was willing to spend more, I have to admit I was the one who finally called it quits. I just had to take a break because I ran out of gas and my knees were really hurting. Try it once; you'll understand just how painful being on your knees for an extended period of time can be. Besides….I had to pee…bad. Ha Ha.

Often, if a customer is really into a particular girl, love, lust, or maybe just loneliness – doesn't matter, he will ask her to sit with him in a booth where he will buy her Lady's drinks, $20 for a small drink or $40 for a little larger Lover's Drink. Although it sounds like a lot, the girl only gets to keep half while the bar gets the other half. Here, as with the garter, the goal is to keep the customer regularly investing in a momentary relationship. The dancer will make it appear he's the center of her universe to keep the drinks flowing. This is a fine line for the dancer to walk. If she drinks too fast, the customer will rapidly come to the realization she's money hungry and walk away after only a couple of drinks. The girl will never see him again, guaranteed. On the other hand, if she drinks too slowly, she won't make as much money as she could have just dancing on the stage. The club management will also quickly become upset, thinking the girl has established a side arrangement with the customer to cheat the bar of profits and will begin sending a waiter around frequently to prime the pump by asking the customer and the girl if they need more drinks. If the correct pace is reached where the customer is enthralled with the girl and she's got him realizing he needs to get her a drink at certain time intervals, she can keep him going until his wallet runs out. If the girl is really lucky, her customer will actually be aware of the required drink pace and will start looking for a waiter when he feels the next drink is due. I've seen girls keep this up with a single guy their entire dance shift of seven hours, I've done it. I have one customer that sits with me the entire night every Friday. Great for me, I don't have to be on stage, great for him because he has my undivided attention. The only downside is it's hard on his finances. Eventually, after he kept up this pace for several months, we reached an agreement where I slow down on the drinks and at the end of the night he makes up the difference in cash. SHHHHH….I didn't say that! Me admitting this is exactly why I don't tell you the real name of the Hot Zone. It would get me fired because in essence I'm cheating the club out of earnings. But I figured at this point, my customer has supported the club enough and I wanted to give him a break. I do have a heart after all. To tell you the truth, I'm not the only girl that does this for their favorite customers. And let me get this straight before we go on further….no, I don't sleep with him, it's a sensible working relationship that saves him money by paying me directly instead of the bar getting half his money (at my expense). This led to other arrangements later on; we called them propositions, where I don't go into the club at all on Saturday nights. He used to also sit with me on Saturday. Now, instead of dancing, I go out with him on a regular date. We eat in nice restaurants, go to clubs and movies, etc. Then he compensates me for the loss of the income I would have gotten by dancing that night. In essence, I'm a paid escort for him, but it's more personal than business, I really like him and he's a lot of fun to be with. It's a win-win for both of us. And again….there's no sex involved; I actually think he likes me for the company and conversation…weird huh? I'll talk more about him later under Sugar Daddy, but he's actually married with his wife who goes on trips for months at a time. I think he's relieved that my insistence of no sex actually removes temptation for him to cheat on his wife. My "no sex" demand wasn't actually a shock to him; I made that very clear right up front. Why? I do not sell my punani to anyone period. It is really the only private thing left in my life that I have control of. Anyone can see every detail of my body in gynecological detail for just a few dollars, but they will never have access to my punani unless I allow it, and believe me it won't be for money. It is my one pillar of self-respect and I cling to it with all the strength I have.

Sorry for going off on that tangent, but it is a point of pride for me. Now getting back to my narration of what goes on in the Hot Zone, besides getting a customer to buy her a Lady's drink, a dancer can also entice him to take her to two more intimate places in the club for a private dance. I say entice, because either place will cost the customer more money for the experience, you can even say one of these places is a significant investment. The Table Dance room is just off the main dance floor. Inside are four small booths that look very similar to library study carrels but the people sitting in these carrels are studying something a little more interesting than books or a homework assignment – a naked dancer in very close proximity. A small wooden bar is latched down across the front of the booth about chest high to prevent the customer from reaching out and touching the girl (or at least that's the concept). One of the club employees also sits on the other side of this small room watching what goes on via small mirrors hanging down from the ceiling in each of the corners of the room. Once the customer is safely ensconced in his booth, the girl will start dancing for him at the start of the next song. The customer has purchased her time for $25 a song, of which the girl and club share 50-50, and a tip for the club employee standing guard inside the room. There is a small ottoman in front of the booth that the girl can use as a prop and you'd be surprised how enterprising we are at using this prop. I have to admit dancing in this setting can be far more sensual than on the larger dancing stages. For one thing, there aren't any idiots standing around behind your customer ogling you as you dance for him; it is one-on-one dancing at its finest. It's not a lap dance, which is illegal, but it's remarkable how close a girl can get to the customer without actually touching him, well maybe touching him sometimes, accidentally, of course. Ha Ha...all in the name of convincing the customer he want more dances. I am very good at sitting on the ottoman, leaning back, and extending a foot into the carrel and letting my toes do the walking...Ha Ha.

The last option for a customer is our Champagne Room located upstairs. This is the Holy Grail that all the girls try to steer their customers towards. Here, for the cost of a bottle of champagne, usually $600 which is sometimes negotiable between the girl and the customer, the customer can be alone with a girl in an even more intimate setting then the Table Dance room. I say the cost of the bottle is negotiable because I have varied it for a customer depending upon how much money I think he has and how much I like him. I've gone as low as $300 at times. How much can you make in the Champagne Lounge? My highpoint is $1000 (two $500 bottles). I've seen several occasions where a girl made up to $6000, but I think that is still cheap when you compare our charges with similar clubs in Las Vegas or New York. But to temper the enthusiasm of the moment, when a girl gets a customer upstairs, like the Table Dance room, the bar gets a 50% cut of the profit. Besides the cost of the champagne, there is also a $20 bar charge which I make the customer pay. Some girls will pay this charge themselves out of their earnings but I'm not that stupid. What do the customers get for their money? Some girls, well most, promise the guy they'll get their money's worth in sensual delights. If your idea of sensual delights is sitting on a couch (instead of a library carrel) and watching a girl dance naked, then OK, the Champagne Room is a place you need to go to. But, despite what thrills the girls promise, the rules are the same, NO TOUCHING, and there are cameras in the room to make sure that doesn't happen. I try not to be dishonest when talking to a customer about the Champagne Room and sometimes I just flat tell a customer he'll end up being disappointed. See I do have some morals! But I have to say, sometimes the temptation of the money is just too great and I make the sales pitch for all it's worth…I guess there go my morals. Ha Ha. The real artistic part of this whole deal is how the girl makes an exit when the guy realizes he's spending a large sum of money and not getting his fantasies fulfilled. You can see their change in attitude the very second their brains processes the fact they're going to go home broke and unsatisfied. I don't blame them and when they start to complain that's my cue to quickly leave and hide. I'll collect my money when I see them walk out of the club. Do I feel bad? Sometimes….not always. They're adults and the decision to go to the Champagne Room is all theirs. The only problem is it was their little head making the decision and when their big head finally gets control of the situation they get angry. Chances are you'll never see that customer again. I say the chances are, because I do have customers who repeatedly come back and take me upstairs no matter how little they get in return. I guess it's my stunning personality…Ha Ha.

Honolulu hosts the NFL Pro Bowl in February every year, and we get a large number of very rich football players coming in expecting special treatment. I also see movies stars expecting the same. But the club owner always refuses their requests for special favors. Although I don't agree with a number of things about the club, I do agree with the no special favors policy and mentally tip my hat to the owner each time I see one of these "special" people walk out the door with an unexpected refusal ringing in their ears. The owner also posts a sign during the Pro-Bowl week saying any dancer caught going home with a football player will be fired, no exceptions. Again, a tip of the hat to the owner. His bottom line is no scandal, nothing illegal…. EVER…. that will put the club at risk of being shut down by the police and rightfully so. The Hot Zone has never been raided by the police or liquor commission. I think this is a testimony for how much they respect the owner of the club and how closely he observes the law…or keeps their pockets well greased.

Before I start talking about the different personalities of the dancers I work with and the customers we strive to please, I think some of the club employees need to be introduced because, in a way, they're also important to the success of the club and to my success as a dancer. First, the DJ, ah yes the DJ, God in his own mind. In this club, he is a combination of DJ and floor manager. He walks around the club frequently like a petty tyrant to ensure enough girls are on stage and aren't sitting around smoking or joking with customers for free. About every 20 minutes or so, he gets on the microphone and announces that girls are needed on such and such a stage because the stage is empty or in danger of being empty because a number of the dancers are doing Lady's drinks or taking a bathroom or smoke break. He has such a whinny, nasally voice which makes all of his announcements very irritating and of course the girls really hustle to occupy the empty stage right after his announcement. NOT!!! That was sarcasm folks. He's a presence to be tolerated, period, and the type of music he plays sucks. I want to tell him…Dude…you're 40 years old and a DJ in a strip club…do you're really think you're a model of success in this life? Again…sarcasm if you don't recognize it. I said earlier if the DJ would make the music slower and more sensual, we dancers would do much better making money. Loud hip-hop music just doesn't seem to do it as a romantic scene setter…maybe in the dance clubs, but not here. How about a little slow and sensual R&B? Someone introduced me to 70's soul music a while back. It was way before my time, but damn, it is sexy.

You would think the DJ and the managers would be all about keeping the girls happier because when it comes right down to it, we're their meal ticket. It's really simple math, no dancers equals no business. But they don't listen to us, in fact they're so jaded from seeing us dancers naked every night they overlook the fact we're even human beings. I had a friend who had the temerity to complain because the club was cold and she was shivering in her skimpy outfit. She wanted to wear a light sweater when she wasn't dancing; she would, of course, take it off quickly when she had a customer. The DJ told her the sweater wasn't permitted under any circumstances and NO they wouldn't turn up the temperature. She quit and the club lost a valuable asset. Was the club concerned that she quit? Nah…there are always plenty of other dancers. That perspective makes the rest of us dancers really feel wanted and really want to work hard for the benefit of the club. Again…that's sarcasm. Ha Ha.

Waiters are a critical part of a dancer's life in the club, in a sense the waiter and the dancer act as a team. A good waiter can help a dancer make a lot of money by keeping her customers well lubricated with liquor and keeping them buying Lady's drinks at a steady pace. A dancer may hesitate to ask a customer for another Lady's drink because she doesn't want to look money-hungry, but the waiter can do the asking for her and can be insistent about it. How can he be insistent? You'd be surprised how compelling it can be when a waiter walks by your table every five minutes asking the customer if he want to buy the lady another drink. The customer will eventually buy the drink or leave (thereby not wasting any more of the dancer's time). This is critical to your success and if the waiter is slow or forgets about you, you lose money. I've been known to lose patience with a slow waiter and go directly to the bartender myself for my Lady's drinks. Of course, that earns me glares from both the bartender and the waiter. You know what? I don't give a fuck, I'm in a business and Lady's drinks are money in my pocket. A good waiter is also Johnny-on-the-Spot with lots of dollar bills in hand to make change for a customer who wants to see you dance. Girls: Rule of thumb: if a customer has a lot of dollar bills, and he lets you see them, he'll spend them on you with the right persuasion. He may be thinking incorrectly that he'll get to spend that money on a number of dancers…but your job is to ensure all that money is directly transferred from his pocket into yours. To hell with the other dancers…didn't I just say this was a business? Ha Ha. Very importantly, the waiter will probably be the first club employee to come to the assistance of a dancer if he sees a customer giving her problems such as being a little too free with his hands or arguing about a Lady's drink. For these reasons, if a dancer is smart, she'll build a comfortable working relationship with one or two specific waiters, meaning if she's working they will serve her and her customer. Of course, part of that relationship is the dancer making sure her waiters get tipped well, if not by the customer, than by the dancer at the end of the night. I have two waiters I routinely use and I always make sure they're well taken care of. After all, it's hard for them not to harbor some hostility towards dancers because they see them making so much money night after night for doing little more than taking their clothes off. So I share a little of the wealth with them to soothe those hostilities…at least towards me. Most of the other dancers also see the wisdom in this.

Bartenders are at the top of the food chain that directly affects a dancer's profits. They service the waiters who service the girls who service the customers who buy the Lady's drinks and tip the dancers. If the chain kinks up and slows down, a dancer doesn't make the money she could have been making. See my rant above about circumventing the waiter link in the chain if the waiter too slow for my taste. Whenever a customer buys a Lady's drink for a dancer, he naturally hopes she'll get drunk and go home with him. He can hope all he wants but it's not going to happen. The bartender will look out for the dancer by serving a Lady's drink with little or no alcohol. Sometimes the first drink may be a stiff one just in case the customer wants to sample it to make sure he's getting his money's worth but after that everything is tea or fruit juice with maybe a whiff of alcohol. This can be a two edge sword; however, which makes me very irritated at times. There are occasions when I want a stiff drink and the bartender won't give me one; being half pickled is not a bad state to be in when you're dealing with an asshole customer. Usually a little bitching will get a small concession and I'll get my drink, but one drink later I'm back on the tea. I've been at odds with the Hot Zone's senior bartender since I began dancing in the club. He is a prick to both the girls and customers for some reason. I think he just hates his job and his life. I don't want to get down to personal insults in this book, I want to take the high road and not mention any names, so I won't, but Mr. Lee was a total jerk….oops, did I accidentally blurt out his name? To get around his ass-holiness, I accept the weak Lady's drink he doles out but then ask my customer to buy himself a second drink (hopefully brimming with alcohol), at bar prices – not Lady's drink prices, which I then drink. This is one of those wink-wink situations you can get away with if you have a good working relationship with your waiter, again another argument to always have a regular waiter. They know what I'm doing and go along with it even though they can get in trouble which is why I make every effort to make sure they get tipped well. And the customers really don't mind because, remember, they're trying to get me drunk so I'll go home with them. Right before I started writing this book, I had a big blow out with Mr. Lee, damn I said his name again. At the end of every night, the dancers have to see him to get their share of the Lady's drink money before they go home. He is the keeper of the drink tally. If you remember, the dancer gets half of every Lady's drink she can talk a customer into buying for her; so for you math whizzes, we get $10 for each $20 dollar drink; $20 for each $40 drink, etc. When it comes time for us to get our money from Mr. Lee, damn there's his name again, he invariably cheats us by at least one or two drinks and pockets the difference. Most girls suck it up and write it off as the price of doing business. I usually do too, but for some reason, I was feeling obstinate that night and I called him on it. Well, this was a FACE issue. To an Asian, face is everything; it's like someone questioning your honor, your family history, and your dick size all at once in front of everyone. This was especially serious because he was being questioned by a low-life dancer. A lot of words were said at high volume, the "F" word playing a prominent role in its every grammatical form - noun, verb, adjective, present participle, past participle, and exclamation to name a few. I probably even used it as a gerund, if I knew what the hell that was. I was proud of my inventiveness. FUCK is such a flexible word...FUCK, FUCKED, FUCKING, FUCKEDUP, FUCKYOUAND THE FUCKINGHORSEYOU RODEINONANDYOURFUCKINGDOGTOO. Needless to say, the disagreement made its way to the club manager. No surprise, I think we were so loud everyone in Honolulu heard it. Mr. Lee and I both expected I would get fired so I stormed out of the club (with all of my money of course). Not to let a dying dog go unkicked, Mr. Lee followed me to gloat and relay the message that the club owner wanted to see me. Much to his dismay and my shock I didn't get fired. The boss just told me to calm down and sent Mr. Lee back to the bar with an enormous loss of face. He said he understood why I was upset but strongly implied I would be looking for another job if there any more outbursts from me. After that, Mr. Lee and I make a concerted effort to ignore each other. He gives me my money at the end of the night without saying a word, and in the correct amount. Since then, other dancers have come up to me saying thanks for standing up to Mr. Lee because he was cheating them too but they didn't have the nerve to speak up. I've even seen Mr. Lee smile at the dancers and customers on occasion, so maybe my taking a stand was beneficial in the long run.

Enough about the bartenders, other than Mr. Lee, they're all good guys and I get along with them pretty good. Most of them even smile at me....when Mr. Lee isn't looking. Now let's move on to the bouncers. I'd like to tell you all about them, but unfortunately, there's not a lot to say. They are the biggest guys in the club. I say big…and that's an understatement, they are fucking movie screens with legs and tree trunks for arms…. and they are very intimidating - they need to be to handle drunk or belligerent customers. A customer would have to be very drunk, and very, very stupid to want to take them on and surprisingly enough, there are few just like that. Most of the times the bouncers sit in booths near the stages and flirt with the girls, but there are times when they've been needed, and when they're needed, they are REALLY needed. We had one bouncer get shot a few years ago so I guess their job isn't all roses and ogling naked girls. Because I'm such a small person, I do the same thing with our bouncers that I do with the bouncers in the Waikiki nightclubs. I go around to each of them every night for a little schmoozing to make sure they'll hustle if I have a problem either with a customer or a fellow dancer.

What this all boils down to is at the end of the night, I have to dole out a lot of my earnings in tips before I leave – to the waiters, the DJ, the bartenders, the bouncers, and even the fricking parking lot attendants. This is OK on nights when I make a lot of money. I don't have a problem in sharing the wealth a little, after all they're guys and can't go onstage and make money at will; they just have to make do with their minimum wage life. It really hurts, however, on slow nights when all of the tips drastically cut my take home pay and the rent and other bills are due. But, I can't complain, it's just one of life's little necessities to grease the skids.

The Dancers

Dancers are the engine that drives any strip club. They are the primary reason a club succeeds or fails. It's not the alcohol or the DJ or the waiters that bring in the customers, it's the dancers. You can have the plushest strip club in the city but if the girls are old and ugly, or they can't interact well with the customers, customers will only come in once to check the place out and then never return which is the death knell for any club. The clubs are also not the best place to work whether they're plush Gentlemen's clubs or dives; it's in the nature of the business. Not only is the work degrading, it can also be dangerous on occasion given the fact we have to entertain drunken lust-driven customers. I saw a picture on the Internet that kind of summed up the risk of this work environment. It depicted a cat walking in front of a line of about 14-15 German Shepherds. Although the dogs were letting the cat walk by unmolested, you had the feeling their restraint was tenuous and it wouldn't take much provocation for them to leap on the cat and tear it apart. Another visual – imagine yourself dancing in front of a pride of lions with a costume comprised of strips of meat. The men we dance for are only marginally inhibited by the rules of the club and state laws (remember the no-touching law?). Their observation of these rules and their conduct in general is wholly influenced by the amount of alcohol they drink. In fact, with some customers, these rules and regulations present a challenge for them to see how far they can push the envelope. These customers are exactly the reason why strip clubs have huge bouncers. Truthfully, even today, men are not that far removed from their Neanderthal ancestors who wanted nothing more than to club a woman and drag her twitching body by the hair back to their caves for sex and to clean the game they kill. This type of behavior is only encouraged by their perception of strippers as mindless bodies and sexual provocateurs.

Quite frankly, there is a definite difference between how men and women view strippers. Women go into a strip club to have a good time with their friends and enjoy the titillation of being naughty by ogling buff, naked men. It's all in good fun. With men, it's more primal and less fun. I think a better visual would be my description of a pride of lions staring at a girl in a meat bikini…with mouths watering….and full blown arousals. Get the difference? Women are there for a good time but men would rape and pillage if they could get away with it … with an emphasis on rape. With this in mind, female dancers continually tread a very fine line – dance for the customers to get them sexually aroused so they'll spend money but don't get them so aroused they'll lose all of their inhibitions, especially when they're drinking. I am very skilled a balancing on this fine line which is why I have been so successful. I know instinctively (or maybe from years of dancing experience) what buttons to push for each customer that sits in front of me with the bottom line of profiting from his lusts and fantasies. I also know how to cool a customer down if he gets overheated. For example one of the best ways of doing this is asking about his wife and kids. All I can say is thank God for the bouncers when I miscalculate and push a customer a little too far over the line between acceptable and unacceptable behavior.

I've been stripping for nine years now and have worked with girls of all types, sizes, and outlooks on life. I wrote a paper on Exotic Dancers in one of my college classes a couple of years ago. I discussed how being a stripper is just a job, a way to make money to make ends meet and not always a sign of a morally dissolute lifestyle. I got an A; however, my teacher said the paper would have been better if I had interviewed some dancers to get their personal point of view firsthand. I was floored. I wanted to say, Dude, Hello...I did....I am one you idiot, and I interviewed me! But I didn't, I just took my "A" and moved on to the next class. What was funny was the reaction of my class when my paper was discussed during class. Apparently stripping as an occupation is not a topic commonly discussed in any class. Ha Ha. Whatever comments my teacher had on the validity of my paper, everything I wrote in it was true; most dancers, me included, have families to support and bills to pay. A girl showing up at a PTA meeting because she has a child attending the school might be a stripper at night and you wouldn't even be able to tell. Being a stripper doesn't mean you can't be a great mother too or a great wife to a loving husband (with a very understanding attitude towards his wife getting naked in front of strangers Ha Ha). A lot of people don't realize that, my teacher and classmates certainly didn't.

Even though I say stripping is like other jobs people go to daily, it takes a little more preparation and certainly a lot of internal fortitude – sometimes liquid/drug induced. You see, it's very hard to get naked in front of a lot of men despite what I said earlier about having no problems doing it when I first started dancing. I was young and stupid then and you'd be surprised at what you're willing to do when it comes down to avoiding sleeping in the street and not eating. After all these years, I can dance every night and go home without giving the fact I was naked most of the night much after thought, but the older I get, it's getting harder to get on the stage each night without a little liquid fortification. Usually, I'll bring in a bottle of orange juice laced with vodka as a jump start for the evening and then try to keep a buzz going throughout the night either through Lady's drinks or me buying my own shots.

Now for an informal poll for the ladies reading this book - could you be a stripper? I'll ask this same question later at the end of the book but I wanted you thinking about it now as you read my descriptions of fellow dancers and the customers they dance for. You probably have no problem taking your clothes off for your husband or boyfriend and even posing for them a little, but what about a room full of drunk and horny men? If you think you could, go to the nearest strip club late in the evening and answer the question again. Seeing drunken men crowding around the stages may give you second thoughts about taking your clothes off and spreading your legs. There's a world of difference between doing it for a significant other and for a crowd of men in a club. Standing in the club, you might realize that just applying for a job in a strip club and then walking on stage for the first time are huge mental hurdles every dancer just starting out in the business has to conquer. But getting naked is only just part one of the task, the easy part. Besides being naked, you also have to be sexy. As strange as it sounds, getting naked and being sexy are two different things and customers, especially jaded customers who frequent strip clubs and are very quick in the discernment. If you are just getting naked, customers will get bored after only a few minutes and move on as soon as they've seen your punani, spending as little money as they can get by with to see it. If you want to get more money out of a customer, you have to make them <u>want</u> to stay and being sexual does that. A customer with a raging hard on isn't keen on getting up and moving on for a couple of reasons. First, he doesn't want any of the other men standing around the stage to see he has a raging boner, and second he'll want to sustain the great feeling that gave him the boner in the first place as long as possible. We'll talk more about sexiness at length later in the book. Why? Because you want your customer to feel like he's having sex with you even though he's not allowed to touch you. I think being sexual in front of a large group of drooling men is the most difficult part of dancing and if one of my customers gets up after watching me dance with a big bulge in the front of his pants with a small wet spot on top of it, I get a feeling of a job well done because I know I've gotten into his mind and more importantly, into his fantasies...and made him happy. I'd be willing to bet every dollar I made off of him that this customer will go straight home and whack off with me as the lead actress in his personal porn movie. And best of all, I can almost count on seeing him sitting in front of me again…and again….and again. A repeat customer is goal for every dancer because it's income she can count on.

I said earlier I drink vodka to jump start my dancing nights and yes, deaden the pain of being a stripper and dealing with asshole customers. Other girls have their own way of coping, drinking (like me) or taking drugs are the more popular. I see various dancers coping every time I walk into the lady's bathroom or the dancer's dressing room. I have a friend, a Thai girl who has more of a religious approach. She is a Buddhist and takes a charm out of her purse right before she goes on stage muttering a short prayer in her native language. She looks and acts like she's getting ready to go into battle. I can't disagree with her mental preparation if it puts her in the right mood to dance. What is humorous; however, is the charm looked like a little dick and she calls it her ding-a-ling. She grasps it firmly between her two hands holds it in front of her face and prays. If she were Catholic, it would be a rosary. I don't know what she is praying but it is probably "Lord, help me cope with these idiots tonight." She also has a boyfriend she calls at various times during the night, or who calls her, to keep her grounded. She's always worrying that some of her boyfriend's friends will walk into the club and see her dancing. This is a fear every dancer has, me included, and occasionally, it happens. In one instance, some of my college classmates walked into the Hot Zone one evening while I was dancing. I couldn't avoid them of course, so I made the best of the situation and brazened it out...and yes I danced for them. I couldn't help but thinking; however, that if they were really my friends they wouldn't have embarrassed me by asking me to dance for them. But they were boys really and I don't think polite common sense played a part in their thinking. It was an uncomfortable remaining two weeks of the class. I could feel the eyes on me with smirks on their faces. On those occasions when I have a boyfriend, or someone I particularly care about, I'll be upfront and tell them what I do for a living so they won't wander into the club and be surprised. I'll also ask them to stay out of the club if they don't want to see me dancing for other guys. There are things I have to do while dancing to get customers to spend money on me, things I don't want a boyfriend to see. Somehow telling them it's just business doesn't help. On a couple of occasions, my admission of being a stripper has ended my relationship on the spot, and I didn't have to worry about anything further. (Ha Ha...or poor me?) One of my best friends is an older man who has been my steady customer for four years now. I talked about him earlier and will also discuss him later as my Sugar Daddy (what's a Sugar Daddy? Read on). He sits with me all Friday night and takes me out on Saturdays. We got around him seeing me dance for other customers by having him come in the same time every Friday night. He'll also text me when he's on the way, giving me about a ten minutes heads up. This allows me to finish with a customer before he comes in and be waiting for him in a booth. The guards at the front door know when he's coming and wave him right through without an admission charge; the bartender and our usual waiter also know he's coming and will have his favorite beer waiting for him. Now that is service. But he spends a lot of money here…so it's also good business.

Most of the dancers in the Hot Zone are in the prime of their stripping shelf life - I mean they're young, beautiful, and men want to spend money to see them get naked. That shelf life is only a very brief moment in time, like a flower in full bloom. Depending on the girl, and how well she ages, a good shelf life is between the ages of 21 and 30. After that, she had better age well, like us Asian girls, or have a good steady base of customers or she'll find her income dwindling as she approach the high end of this age group. She also need to begin planning for life after stripping while it's not too late by having a Plan B such as getting a marketable college degree or investing her money wisely. Counting on a rich Prince Charming to ride in on a white horse and marry her is not a valid Plan B, sorry. But believe it or not that is what some of these dancers count on. Dancers in the next age group, 30-35, still have a little life left but they're on the edge and really should be getting ready for life after stripping, in other words they really, really need to have a Plan B well underway. If their income hasn't already begun to suffer, it soon will. Sadly, some dancers in this group still carry on as if they were still in their early 20's, they dance and they party, period. If they have a Plan B at all it's still clinging to the hope of a Mr. Rich Guy marrying them. Most are disappointed and many will eventually settle for a Mr. He'll Do, or a Mr. I Think I Can Train Him. Ironically, all too often they've passed up many opportunities to marry a Mr. Right to wait for a Mr. Rich Guy who never showed up and now never will. After all, if he's rich, why should he settle for an older model stripper when he can get one much younger? Finally, in every bar, you'll see one or two dancers that have hung on way too long, those in the 35-40 range. This is beyond sad, especially if they haven't realized they no longer appeal to customers. They will try to compensate by using thicker layers of makeup and wearing outlandish clothes, but ultimately it's wasted effort. A smart club owner may choose to keep one or two of them on salary as "Mama-sans" for the younger girls. In this capacity, they can relieve the owner and managers of a lot of the headaches of day-to-day management of the dancers and their girl problems (read boyfriend miseries, PMS, petty jealousies, squabbles between dancers, etc). But these older dancers can also cause their own problems if they try too hard to hustle drinks or, God forbid, take their clothes off. There are some exceptions to this "too old" group of women. If you haven't realized it by now, we Asian girls don't show our age as quickly as girls of other nationalities. I don't know why, good genes? Anyway, there are three dancers in the club, a Korean and two Japanese, who are over 40 but still look great and are still bringing in the customers. Guys, take this as a hint. If you want a wife that will continue to look good for many years, think about marrying an Asian girl. If you are rich and good looking, think about marrying me....Ha Ha.

While I'm on the topic of giving you general information before I actually start talking specifically about some of the dancers I work with, I think it would be good to first describe some of the necessary job skills and accessories each dancer needs to succeed. Some are obvious, some not so much so. You can't just walk into a club and take off your clothes, well you can, but you will certainly get arrested if you're not an employee of the club...Ha Ha....or......hired if you are good looking....Ha Ha. Even if you are already an employee and are very good looking, your looks will only take you so far. In other words your looks and willingness to get naked will entice a customer to sit down in front of you and start paying to watch you dance, but you'll need certain job skills and accessories to get his attention and keep him spending with wild abandon long after you've taken off all your clothes and he's ogled your punani from every possible angle every pornographic photographer thought possible. And yes, I'm going to talk about sexiness again...so stand by. I love that phrase "spending with wild abandon." You'll see me constantly referring to that goal throughout this book because that is our bottom line as a stripper....to get (or a better term is entice) customers to drop all of their hard-earned money on us. If the night goes right, they'll go home poor but happy...we dancers just go home happy.

Job Skills and Abilities

Every job requires a set of pre-requisite skills or abilities its employees need to have, or be able to learn quickly, for them to be a success. Stripping is no different. I had previously named this section just "Job Skills", but given what I talk about in the next few paragraphs, that wasn't exactly correct. Most are not tangible, measurable skills like typing so many words per minute. But they're still necessary attributes for a dancer to be successful. As I've said repeatedly, to be successful, a stripper needs to do more than just get naked; in fact, getting naked may be the least part of the job if you want to earn top dollar. I'm going to list a few of the more significant prerequisites I think each prospective stripper needs to have or needs to acquire very quickly. I've mentioned some of them earlier, sexiness for one thing, but I think they're important enough to repeat. Some of these prerequisites can be learned if they're not already innate in prospective dancer, but sadly, there are few if any professional stripper schools to teach them. Dancers mostly have to learn on the fly, honing their skills while they dance. Trial and error....trial and error, finding out what works and, importantly, what doesn't work for a particular girl's dancing style. Some girls never master any of these prerequisites and quickly fade as strippers. And what metric do you use to gauge how well you're mastering these skills? Money...of course, the universal success metric. If you're making a lot of money, you've mastered them, if you're not....then, buckle down and learn or find something else to do.

- *Sexiness*

You knew this was coming because I've beaten the drum on it quite a bit already. Sexiness goes to the heart of what every stripper is supposed to be, a sex goddess, the subject of wet dreams, a walking dose of Viagra. It is one of the central themes of this book and I'm going to test you all on it the back of the book...so pay attention students. Fundamentally speaking, getting naked and being sexy are two different things, apples and oranges. I'll bet you've never made that distinction. Anyone can get naked. We all get naked when we take a shower and change clothes and we aren't particularly sexy while doing them. To me nakedness is a physical condition while sexiness is a state of mind and attitude. I will concede nakedness can set the stage for being sexy but this is not a wholehearted agreement. I think women look far sexier clothed than totally naked. A lot of women...and men will agree with me. Clothing hides flaws and it makes people looking at you use their imagination to guess what you look like naked. And we all know how powerful imagination is and it does a good job of glossing over the flaws. But that said, ladies, if you're naked in front of someone... do something with it...don't just stand there....being naked. Most women think men will find them sexy simply because they're women. That may be true for teenage boys who think with their crotches and see every women they encounter in a sexual context. Hell, they frame everything they see and think about in a sexual context...Ha Ha. That's not totally true for grown men, especially the jaded men I dance for nightly who frequent strip clubs. They can be very discerning when it comes to sexiness and are the first to distinguish between sexiness and nakedness. You can't see, taste, or smell sexiness but you sure as hell know it's there. It's an arousal trigger that probably strikes at some prehistoric vestige in our souls. Some women are born with a sexy gene in their DNA. These lucky women ooze an innate sexuality that both men and women are instantly aware of. Some scientist will tell you these women send out pheromones like a garden sprinkler making men babble because their dicks are dominating their thought processes. These "sex bombs" could be modestly covered from head to toe in a burkha surrounded by family members and still make Arab men want to stone them for inappropriate behavior. You can detect the presence of a sexy gene even in little girls as young as two years old. These are the flirts who have absolutely no fear of talking to men or showing these men the cute lamb on their panties right in front of Daddy. They know they're cute and don't hesitate to use that cuteness to get what they want. They are the cheerleaders and prom queens in high school. They are the girls who have male groupies hanging around them in school or work. Get the picture? Want a visual? Angelina Jolie…enough said. Hell, I'd make a run at her. So you can see how being sexy can help a stripper or help a wife keep an active sex life with her husband. Although I've stated some people are born sexy, it can also be a learned skill, something that can be practiced in front of a bedroom mirror or in front of a significant other. As step one, learn to get rid of your inhibitions. Don't be shy about your body or your sexual feelings. Women do get horny, so why cover that fact up? Open desire is very sexy and a great come on. Think of the most sexually perverted thing that first comes to mind...and then do it. Well....providing the first thing that comes to mind isn't having sex with your pet...forget it then....you're sick. Ha Ha. As a stripper, I want the customer sitting in front of me sporting a hard on before I've even taken off a single article of clothing. I want him sweating and stammering when he tries to talk to me. I want to see a wet spot in the front of his pants when he leaves. I want to haunt his memories and wet dreams long after he gets home, because if I accomplish that, I've gained a repeat customer that will come back, and back, and back......who will spend and spend and spend. Ha Ha.

- *Ability to Dance*

Well DUH! This is a basic job skill. If you think of stripping at all, chances are you visualize a stripper actually dancing on a stage taking her clothes off in rhythm to the music being played, or gracefully dancing around a stripper pole. You can probably even hum a number of "stripper" songs if you're into stereotypes....*She's a Maneater*...hmmmm. Some girls actually do use the stripper poles on each stage in the Hot Zone and I'll describe them later under acrobats, but I don't. If you want to know the truth, I don't "dance" at all in the strictest definition of the word dance. I'm not even sure I quality for a loose definition of dancing. A lot of the girls in the Hot Zone don't either, so maybe I should have entitled this section *"Have Some Basic*

Coordination." Why don't we "dance" in the conventional fashion? Because that takes a lot of energy when you're on stage for eight hours. Also, we like to get more intimate with our customers, so we just sit or kneel on a cushioned pad right in front of them, getting as close to them as the stage will allow. We then do different sensual poses in time with the music being played trying to get our customers sexually aroused. Each dancer has her favorite poses which she knows will best show off her body. If you're looking for adjectives to describe my "dancing" I would say languid, smooth, unhurried, feline, etc. I very rarely get totally naked, using the different parts of my costume as props. Eventually my clothes do come off, my shorts and bra being the first to go, but I like to keep my g-string on as long as possible, pulling it aside occasionally to reward a customer with a short glimpse of my punani after he's been a good boy and put a number of dollars into my garter promptly when asked and with no complaining. Amazing as it sounds, you can train customers….kind of like Pavlov's dogs….Ha Ha…complete with drooling. I think teasing is a lost art, but that's why this profession used to be called "Strip Tease"; it's something I do well to my financial advantage. It's how a woman teases her lover, or should tease him to keep his interest up. My poses, body movements, and sexual attitude, pull my customers out of their mundane lives and into a fantasy world where we're lovers preparing to have the best sex in our lives. It's a feeling they want to sustain as long as possible, no matter how much money they have to spend to do it. Sound like a lot of bullshit? Not really. I do it many times every night and am very good at it. It's a point of pride for me, giving a customer the best thrill for his money. I'll bet you didn't think a stripper could have pride in her work did you? I should be a saint...St. Amaya...the bringer of inner peace and raging boners for my customers. The demolisher of impotence. Ha Ha. Maybe one of my dancing outfits should be a nun's habit...Ha Ha....remember that when I talk about costume themes under accessories a little later. A nun's costume is all black and austere on the outside but with a sexy chewable center. I am so going to Hell, in fact they are probably designing a whole new wing in Hell just for my tortures. Ha Ha. But I digress yet again...having basic dancing or coordinated movement skills are often how you can tell the difference between a dancer that's just starting out and one that been dancing for a while. This skill can be the difference between a stripper just getting by or one making a lot of money.

- *Attitude*

I struggled to find a proper place to discuss attitude because it's a very broad topic with many facets. I listed it first under accessories which I'll be talking about next but it didn't quite fit because it's not a physical thing you can touch or feel like clothes or jewelry. It doesn't really fit under job skills in the traditional sense either because when you think about job skills you think of typing and writing skills, or being able to fix a computer. No, attitude isn't any of these things, but it is as essential to being a successful stripper as having the right costume or the right make up. So I really wanted to talk about it. It's the armor any performer in the public eye needs to have to survive, from the most famous movie actress to us strippers. And strippers need it more than actresses, because when you're nude in public there's nowhere to hide, Dude. Anyone who takes their clothes off for a living has to "wear" a kick ass take no prisoners attitude as a shield against the lustful alcohol-soaked idiots they dance for every night. And you're certainly going to get a lot of "holier than thou" attitude from many customers and from the club staff who look down on you as "just a stripper" and will treat you accordingly. I have an attitude, I admit it. I am THE Queen Bitch, the star of your wet dream fantasies. Someone better than the customers and certainly better than my fellow dancers. I've have a lot of people wish me good luck before I start working. My response is I don't need luck, I know I will make my money no matter how bad business is for the rest of the dancers. Attitude? You betcha! I'm always confident in my appearance and in my ability to get and keep customers and that confidence attracts customers. I guess they feel confident dancers will not be too shy to sexually entice and shamefully arouse their lust and fantasies. And when a customer tries to show me attitude? All I can say is "Beware of the Force." Ha Ha.

Now that I've given you my dissertation on having an attitude to be successful as a stripper, let me throw in a couple of qualifiers to my basic definition. Having a Queen Bitch attitude is fine, especially in dealing with fellow dancers or with asshole club employees, but it's not necessarily the best thing to throw at all of your customers. Sure, if you find yourself dealing with a pervert or a pompous jerk, then by all means out attitude him…but, for the normal customers a little modification to the Queen Bitch is called for if you want to keep them as a customer. This is a very fine line you have to maneuver around. Having too much attitude, being too cocky, turns customers off. Go too far, and you're suddenly the hard hearted stripper portrayed in the movies, someone to avoid if you don't want to be cheated out of your money. So you ask, what do I do St. Amaya?.....Well……my daughter let me enlighten you.

- Vulnerability

One of the first things to consider in tempering your attitude is to show a little vulnerability. It seems contradictory to talk about attitude and vulnerability in the same sentence, but they coexist well, and not only is combining the two doable, it's very effective.

Vulnerability is very appealing to customers. It works to make your armor not quite so impenetrable, it softens your Queen Bitch image to make you more approachable and likable. By definition, being vulnerable makes you seem capable of being physically or emotionally wounded. Or it could mean something bad already happened to you and you're a little damaged by it. Men love that, it brings out their primitive need to protect a woman or to perceive a problem and try to fix it and the very fact that you are otherwise a Queen Bitch, makes your vulnerabilities all the more visible and irresistible to react to. Both drive me nuts in my personal life, but they're pure gold when I'm working with a customer. It's like -

"Oh, you feel bad? Well here's some money to cheer you up Sweetheart". Of course my response is effusive gratitude which results in more money springing out of my customer's wallet. This is a lesson all you wives and girlfriends can apply towards your significant other. Want or need something? Just look like the lack of that something is hurting you emotionally. It will appear like magic...Ha Ha. Whatever floats men's boats....

- *Smiling*

Smiling is another attitude modifier you need to employ. Everyone needs to smile more; it makes the people you're smiling at feel good, and in the stripping business, making your customers feel good can only be profitable for you. It can be the most insincere smile in history, but it's still a smile. Even if your current boyfriend left you and the neighbor's dog ate your cat...S M I L E. Why? Just put yourself in the shoes of a customer. Would you want to watch a girl dance with a constant grimace on her face as if she just farted, or who appears to be thinking you were less than the dirt on her shoes? If you say yes, then you're a sick person. Into whips and domination much? As a dancer, I want my customer feeling welcome and a big welcoming smile on my face certainly helps. A big, SINCERE, welcoming smile....a lot of times you have to give an academy award performance...but so what? Just visualize the big, yellow WalMart happy face that keeps smiling no matter what type of strange customer comes through their doors, and WalMart gets their share of strange (Wal-Martians) just like dancers do, maybe more so. I've seen plenty of customers I'm sure were just a short step ahead of the butterfly net or a police vice squad but I still managed to smile while I danced for them…all the while hoping they wouldn't climb onto the stage. Looking at these experiences positively, maybe my smile was the first nice thing they've ever seen or seen in a long time. Smiling means acceptance, something they probably have trouble getting even from their relatives. My thinking is, smiling is painless and it may be just the right nudge to get a customer to open up his wallet or to walk out of the club with a more positive outlook on life. Cost of therapy session with me? About $20, cheap at triple the price. The doctor is now in…Ha Ha.

- *Thick skin*

What do I mean by thick skin? I define it as imperviousness to having your feelings hurt. I guess it's another layer of armor for you in addition to the attitude. Again using the actress analogy, people in the public eye can be subjected to all source of abuse some of it pretty direct and brutal. Although you won't see our pictures coupled with a story of an illicit love affair in a grocery store gossip magazine like you do movie stars, we're still out there in the public eye in front of an unforgiving, drunk audience…and as I said before…naked. If we're too fat or too thin we're going to hear insults. If our breasts are too small…or aren't as firm as they should be…insults. If we have a mole or a pimple somewhere….yeah, you guessed it…insults. So we really need very thick skin because we are absolutely not going to please everyone…it's the nature of the beast. Trying to live up to someone's fantasy can be very tricky and unrewarding at times. Going along with the movie star analogy, think of our detractors as movie critics…only drunk and more stupid…just the type of people we have to face every night.…Ha Ha. A dancer could be the most beautiful creature on God's earth and still hear some little shit nitpick on her appearance or attitude. Sometimes you'll hear a woman critique a dancer harshly to a boyfriend or husband just to make herself look better in his eyes. And that's OK…she's protecting her turf…it's just business. If he's not an idiot, he'll agree with her. But he'll be a bigger idiot to keep insisting on dragging her to strip clubs. But enough about that right now, I'll talk more about it later. Having a thick skin can be either be a natural or learned trait; a lot of dancers just never seem to acquire one, they're sensitive to insults or perceived slights and their feelings get bruised easily. They don't last long. What types of slights do we see a lot? Customers are a fickle lot and I get passed by all the time by a customer wanting another dancer to entertain him. A sensitive person would feel rejection. Me, being the hard shelled bitch I am, realize it's just business. If you've been a dancer for any length of time, you learn very quickly to not take these rejections personally. The fact they passed me by is not personal, it's more likely I was simply not their type, i.e. the girl of their fantasies. A lot of customers come into the club looking for a specific type of a girl, for example, a blond dancer (when I have black hair) or some other attribute that I have absolutely no chance of satisfying. That means their rejection of me is totally out of my control, so why worry about it? Some people buy Fords, some buy Chevrolets...personal choice is all it is. However, if someone comes into the club looking for a petite, but voluptuous Filipino dancer...then here I am and those blond bitches can just suck my dick. Or they may be less specific and are just looking for an Asian dancer... again...here I am, especially if they have a lot of money to spend.

Being impervious to insults is another benefit of having a thick skin. As you dance, you can hear some pretty personal and insulting comments on your body and looks slurred loudly by drunken customers. Even with my rhinoceros quality thick skin, these remarks can cut deep. I've been called a whore just because I asked a customer to put more money into my garter. I've been called a whore and bitch because I rejected a customer's request for a date. I frequently hear comparisons of my various body parts with those of other dancers, some are very favorable but others are mean and hurtful. And customers aren't the only source of insulting remarks or insulting treatment. We get it a lot from the club staff who think they're better than the dancers and are jealous of the money we make. I'd like to see them dance naked......on second thought...nah! But through it all, I act professionally and keep a poker face as if the remarks are meaningless to me, all the while wishing the God of Castration pays a visit to the jerk who made the remarks. Too extreme? I think the customers and club staff would be more than shocked if they could hear what the girls say about them. Ha Ha. I think lack of penis size enters the discussions quite a bit. I hope they have thick skins too…Ha Ha.

- *Talking and Listening*

This job skill might sound counterintuitive when you consider the main focus of our job is taking our clothes off. Ok...you have a point. BUT….like all of the other job skills I'm discussing, being able to engage a customer in a conversation, or just being willing and able to listen while he talks can keep a customer paying for your services long after you've shed all your clothes and he's ogled even the most private corners of your body. I talked about this earlier in the book at length, but I think it's such an important point, it's worth repeating. Some girls never learn how to talk to customers, or don't want to, and they lose a lot of potential income because of this. I've found most customers want to talk, some painfully so. Other than seeing naked women, loneliness is probably the strongest motivator that brings men into the Hot Zone. Hostess Bar girls figured this out a long time ago and are experts at talking to their customers despite not always having a firm grasp on English or having great looks. And these Hostesses get a lot of return customers even though they DON'T take their clothes off.   I will talk more about this later when I discuss types of customers, the lonely customers in particular. You're probably asking why customers even want to talk to us? Simple answer, we're available, non-judgmental, sympathetic, and as long as they keep paying, a captive audience. And <u>we know how to listen</u> after years of talking to customers. Asian girls are particularly good at this for some reason. A popular saying I've heard is "no man is an island." This is true even though I've observed every man I've ever met trying to be an island. That is just not healthy. They bottle their feelings up internally and become walking potential heart attacks because they have no one to talk. I have a simple remedy for this. A little alcohol, a few gentle prompting words coupled with some gentle caresses on their face and arms and like a dam bursting customers start telling me the most intimate details of their lives, things they would never dream of telling their friends or even their wives or girlfriends - if they had wives and girlfriends. Some have very limited social skills, too limited to even be able to meet and talk to a girl in a normal social setting (read....NOT the Hot Zone). Even sadder is the fact some <u>do</u> have wives or girlfriends and yet here they sit....in front of me. What's so good about me? At the risk of sounding egotistical, I'm not stupid and I pride myself on being able to talk intelligently on any number of subjects, or to sound intelligent talking about them. I know how to ask the right questions that will get a customer talking about his job or himself. Ladies, this is something I bet you don't even try with your husbands. How do I know? Because they're sitting in front of me night after night instead of you spilling their guts about how hard their day was at work or how no one understands them. DUH! I have absolutely no problem being buck naked as they spill their guts. Ladies, maybe you should try that also...Ha Ha. Or, ladies, how about once in a while asking your significant other..."Hon, how was your day?" I've seen pictures of a lot of families. Customers will whip pictures out their wallets at the drop of a hat without even considering the irony of the fact they're showing them to a naked stranger in a place they shouldn't even be in. Ironically, they'll brag about their wives while they're staring at my punani. Sometimes I really want to ask why they aren't with their families instead of being with me in the club, but I don't because the fact they're in the club speaks volumes….something is missing at home. As I said before, we strippers are a valuable social service…Ha Ha. Sometimes I feel like Lucy Van Pelt giving therapy sessions to Charlie Brown. I wish I knew how many people have walked out of the Hot Zone with a much better mental attitude than when they came in after talking to me or any of the dancers for a while. I also like to think that by talking to me, they build the necessary interaction skills to actually talk to a non-stripper in a more socially acceptable setting or God forbid, to their significant others. You can think of me as an advanced teacher in inter-personal skills. Ha Ha. I also hope they leave with much, much tighter pants in the crotch area…Ha Ha. Maybe they'll go home and jump lustfully on their significant others after seeing me. That would be a great conversation starter and it might even help resolve whatever domestic issues they're having. So I'm a marriage counselor too….Ha Ha. For those customers that don't have a significant other but are just as lonely - Dude, find someone….really. I'm told there is someone in this world for everyone, you just need to get out and look….and TALK TO THEM. Hint talking to a stranger isn't hard…you start off by saying Hello and go from there. Sorry…....I think lonely people are one of the saddest facets of our society. One thing not to include in an opening conversation is that your stripper sent you….Ha Ha.

- *Equal Measures of an Open Mind, Cynicism, and Patience*

This job skill goes hand in hand with the Talking and Listening skills discussed above. As I said earlier, customers will talk to you as you dance, some more than others. And as they get more alcohol into their systems, their stories can sometimes get pretty bizarre. Sometimes you'll have doubts whether or not some of your customers are even from this planet or dimension. I don't know how many customers have informed me in all seriousness they were married to me or we were lovers in a former life, with the implication being, of course, they'd like to continue with the relationship in this life, especially the sex Ha Ha. Some can be very convincing or convincing in their minds and are absolutely astounded when I gently turn them down. One of my better customers tries to explain the disparity in our ages (I'm just a little past 30 and he's over 60) by telling me we were indeed married in a former life, only I killed him and that's why he reincarnated so much earlier than I did. I'm thinking the killing was justified. There are others who, I hear words coming out of their mouths, but honest to God, I have no concept of what they're saying. The words are either pure gibberish or just seem to be a series of random words strung together with no real meaning. Maybe I'm so sexy I have them babbling, a nice thought, but I seriously doubt it. More likely, they're not firing on all cylinders. As I said earlier, they're one short step ahead of a butterfly net. I have a good friend who used to work in a government agency that investigated nut letters sent to high ranking government officials. He said one person in particular would write a multi-page letter once a week with color drawings describing the visions he received from Venusians of various foreign military bases. Some of my customers aren't far from this distinctive level of nuttiness. They just can't seem to differentiate fantasy from reality, yet here they are in front of me, most holding jobs and driving on our roads. Dude! When I get a customer like this, I'll dance for him but I'll keep one eye on his body language and another eye on the nearest exit from the stage, ready to bolt at a moment's notice. I can be off the stage and standing next to a bouncer in a heartbeat if I see a customer getting crazy, you know, Barbie doll up the rectum crazy. I am also very careful to nod my head at the appropriate places and say "yes" or "I understand" or just "Hmmmm" which is a very flexible response that can be used on any occasion. What I don't say is "Dude, you're nuts", or "what the fuck are you talking about?" If they appear harmless and put dollar bills into my garter when asked, then what the hell, I'm happy to dance for them crazy or not.

Along with the weirdness, I hear more than my share of bullshit from customers trying to impress the hell out of me. These customers aren't crazy, they just have so little self esteem they have to make up things about themselves they think will impress me. Crazy people are sad, bullshit artists are pathetic. I don't know how many have told me they work for the CIA and aren't allowed to tell me what type of work they do. And they tell me this in a low tone of voice, almost whispering so they can't be overheard, all the while looking back and forth rapidly as if checking for spies, people listening in, etc. I know they expect me to be intrigued and sexually aroused, but it's all I can do to keep from laughing. But I accept everything they tell me with the seriousness they expect out of me, putting an appropriately awed look on my face, and saying "wow" a lot. I don't want to tell them I have met real CIA employees as well as FBI and Secret Service agents. Yes, Secret Service, we get a few into the club every time the President comes to the islands. None of these real agents make a big deal of their jobs or try to impress me with any details; they're professionals and act like it. If you really want to be impressed, you need to meet some SEALS. SEAL is an acronym standing for Sea, Air, and Land. They're the Special Force of the Navy and they are truly impressive people – quiet, competent, handsome with great bodies, and very lethal, ask Osama. And did I say they have great bodies? A lot of them could make a fortune being a male stripper…I'd put money in their thongs. Wooo Hooo!!!!

- A Sense of Humor

Nothing can open a customer's wallet up faster than you having a sense of humor and laughing at their jokes. I see a lot of customers who seem tense when they first sit down in front of me. I'm not sure why they're tense, I don't think I'm all that intimidating, I'm only 4'11". Maybe they just had a bad day or maybe it's because they don't go into strip clubs often or they're not used to being in close proximity of a girl who is willing to get naked for them. Some probably haven't had many meaningful conversations with women at all. Having a sense of humor and a willingness to joke with customers or laugh at their jokes (even if you don't get them) is a great ice breaker. Being willing to laugh goes hand in hand with the other conversational art skills I list in this section of the book. If you laugh at a customer's jokes it makes you seem human and less stand-off-ish, which sad to say, is an attitude adopted by a lot of strippers. Joking immediately puts a customer at ease and lets him feel he has a relationship with you, making him more willing to pay to keep talking to you. There is a very fine edged sword at play here; however. You need to make sure your customer also has a sense of humor and he doesn't think you're laughing at him rather than with him. If I get a customer who is very defensive and humor-deficient which some men just are (the assholes), I'll try a few jokes to loosen him up. If that doesn't work I change my goal to just getting the most money out of him as quickly as possible and then getting rid of him. My work is hard enough without having to please an asshole. But happily, these types of customers are few and far in between. Most genuinely want to laugh with you and have a good time. I've even seen our bartender, Mr. Lee, you know the one I had the yelling match with, smile every once in a while….no…that's not right…once, maybe?…but so what? At least it proves he's human and not the total asshole all the dancers think he is. See, I can be nice.

- *A Good Memory*

Every man on this earth likes to think he's made a strong enough impression on a girl that she'll remember him the next time they meet. Wanting to be memorable is a universal human weakness, it appeals to our ego. All good salesmen practice remembering names and faces because it puts them in good stead with a client right away if they can walk up to the client and say Hi Stan or Hi Dave instead of "excuse me, what was your name again?" I learned that lesson selling cars. The same applies with dancers because in essence, we're all salespersons and we're the product we're trying to sell. If you can remember the name of a customer and what you talked about the last time you danced for him, you're money. He will light right up when you say "Hello Rob" or "Hello John" or whatever he told you his name was (a lot of the really insecure use strip club aliases). I can guarantee he'll immediately feel you're a friend and will spend money to resume the conversation you had the last time you danced for him. The fact someone remembers their name may be a new feeling for some of our customers; the fact that a pretty dancer remembers their name can be a religious experience. If you've ever traveled anywhere in Asia you'll know Asian bargirls are famous for this. I have friends who travel extensively in the Far East and swear they can buy a few drinks for a bar girl one year and she'll remember their name even if they come back a year later. You just can't beat that for hospitality and comfort, it's like coming home. I've always had a good memory for faces and names and I take advantage of that whenever I work. When I'm not dancing, I'll walk around the club and say hello to all of the customers I know calling them by name. It's not surprising that many of these brief encounters end up with the customer buying me a drink or engaging my services on the stage or even better, in the Table Dance room. Easy money. It's like selling brownies to a chocolate addict.

- *Flexibility*

I decided to add this section at the last minute as I was proofreading this book. I don't mean the gymnastic kind of flexibility where a girl puts her legs behind her head...so get your minds out of the gutter. An unusual physical flexibility would certainly get you noticed as a nude dancer, in fact it would make you damn popular. We have a couple of bitch dancers who could probably eat themselves if they wanted to and they have customers lining up to watch them. Did I say bitches? Oops...I guess I lost my objectivity...they have a skill I don't have so to me, they're bitches. Ha Ha. I'm about as flexible as an iron rod. So...that's why I wanted to limit this discussion to mental flexibility. Again, going back to the analogy of speed dating where you're confronted with new faces, new expectations, and new discussions every few minutes, that's exactly how I feel about dancing. One customer leaves and another takes his place like clockwork with no two being the same. I described it as an assembly line in the front of the book because that's what it sometimes feels like. It would be an easy fallback for you to just repeat the conversation you had with a previous customer when someone new sits in front of you. Sometimes that works, but often it doesn't. Oh sure, you can start off with the basics such as "How are you?", "What is your name", and "Where are you from." But then, where do you go once that ritual is done? I guarantee you, if a customer wants to talk at all; it will be a totally different discussion your previous customer. You need to be able to go with the flow and respond intelligently to what he is saying. If they're quiet you may have to try different icebreaking techniques to get him engaged. If they refuse to talk at all other than non-committal grunts then you need to be flexible enough to work with just that. I don't get the grunters often, thank God. I will say that having to accommodate so many types of customers has really improved my mental flexibility, giving me the ability to communicate with people from all walks of life, something I'll emphasize in a resume when I apply for a non-stripping job, although I won't say where I got this skill from for obvious reasons…Duh! Who said strippers are dumb? Ha Ha. As I said earlier, I have a BSIT…...bitch!!! Ha Ha.

Accessories

The job prerequisites and skills I discussed above were primarily personality and attitude – centric. They are not immediately measurable or quantifiable, but nevertheless are major contributors to the success of a stripper or for anyone in a relationship. Accessories on the other hand are more material. When you think of accessories, hats, gloves, shoes readily come to mind. I'll talk about some of these, shoes in particular. We'll also talk about accessories that are not so apparent such as beauty (yes, I call it an accessory), a good body, costumes, make up, hair, and perfume. These are not classically thought of as accessories but I consider them necessary enhancements that strippers need. We're also going to talk about tattoos and piercings. I didn't want to label them as accessories because they're not mandatory; options might be a better term or accessory phenomena I've noticed over the last few years which can hurt a dancer's business if taken to the extreme. Besides neither didn't seem to neatly fit anywhere else, so please bare with me.

- Beauty

Beauty is something most people wouldn't call an accessory, but I do. I'm going to take a lot of heat for this statement, but here it is: being good looking is an important (critical even) necessity to be a successful stripper. I'm sorry ladies, you can have the best body in the world but you won't get much business if you have a face only a mother would love. I'm not going to even try and soften the blow by being politically correct and calling some women "beauty challenged." Ugly is ugly and in an occupation where success is based primarily on a male customer base willing to spend money, being ugly or even plain looking is not a key to success. Men are primarily visual creatures. I'll propose later they're also susceptible to certain smells too, but that's later and beside the point. I will argue with anyone who says visual esthetics doesn't come first with men. To be successful, a dancer must appeal to the fantasies of a customer whose wife is probably not the best looking woman in this earth. So this customer expects to see a naked, beautiful 10 dancer to fuel his fantasies. You don't have to be stunningly beautiful, although I've seen a lot of dancers who are, but you do have to be attractive. Having a girl-next-door attractiveness is a real plus. Looking like you're under aged jailbait is a definitely a big PLUS. And if you wear school girl costumes…Money….Ha Ha. Yeah, the pervert factor is alive and well in the stripping profession, but you all knew that, I'm just confirming it. Wait until we talk more about costumes.

You will see girls who weren't blessed with good looks trying to make a living by stripping but they won't be in the best clubs where the real money is. They'll be in the lesser clubs, like the one I started stripping in where the only way they're able to make money is by letting customers take personal liberties such as groping their boobs or pussies. These are the types of clubs that have small dark rooms in the back for that purpose and they're dark for a reason. This is a sorry existence and the girls in these clubs better off finding another way to make a living. Sadly, a lot of these types of girls in Hawaii are immigrants with very little formal education and barely able to communicate in English, so there aren't many other options for them.

- *Good Body*

A number of you will probably want to argue with me about what is more important for a stripper, a beautiful face or a great body. I rank beauty first because I think it's the most important. But I'm a female. A man might say put a bag over her head and let me enjoy the body. Hmmm. Nah, that's stupid, sorry men. A beautiful stripper can make a lot of money even if she has a so-so body which I define as having small boobs and butt. A woman with a tight, athletic body is very attractive but she probably won't out earn a beauty queen. But if you combine a beautiful face with a great body you will have a VERY POPULAR dancer. One thing top-of-the line dancers can't be is fat. Again, I'm going to climb back into the hot water with this statement. Fatties need not apply, at least not in the nicer clubs, even if you have a good looking face, big boobs, and a big butt. But since pussy is pussy, there's always a market for anything female in some of the lower level strip clubs. It also might work for that small niche of customers who like big women. As an aside, I've found there is a niche for any kind of sexual fantasy, or should I say dysfunction. Actually to be completely cynical, having three eyes and no teeth would appeal to a small niche market...yeah, they're out there. But the same business rule applies for all of these niche markets, you can't be successful in any business if you don't appeal to a broad customer base. A small group of niche customers just won't provide that. As a general rule for the large market of regular strip bar customers, they know exactly what type of women they like, and they won't spend their hard earned money on someone they find unattractive or unappealing. But I digress. I'm petite with a very toned, hard body (I've been bragging about it all through this book if you've been paying attention). I've got a great God-given ass which I'm happy to say I get a lot of complements on. To brag about all my Filipina sistaz' a little, we all have great, God-given booties. I admit, however, I have engineered boobs that my doctor specifically matched to my body size.

Great boobs are almost a necessity for any stripper to be successful. This is a competitive industry and you can't compete if all of the girls dancing around you have big boobs. Telling a customer he should like your small boobs because they're "natural" and therefore anatomically better just didn't seem to hack it so I got new boobs a few years ago. My natural boobs were small but by no means unattractive and I was doing OK without them, but I think I got an inferiority complex looking at all the augmented girls around me on the dance stage. Having large boobs seems to be something all women are considering now, not just movie stars and strippers. They make you look hot when you're out nightclubbing in a tight party dress. But I have just one word of caution, it hurts like hell to have them done and I had a very good surgeon. I got them almost by accident, it was certainly not an event planned well in advance. I was visiting a doctor's office on a day off asking about prices and procedures and the doctor said he had an opening the next day and would I like to come in? Then, he played dirty and gave me a great price. How could I resist? The next day I was getting new boobs. The doctor took a great approach. He didn't ask what cup size I wanted; instead, he showed me snapshot book of previous patients and asked me to pick out the look I wanted, kind of like boob mug shots. I did and we were off to the races. I had a very close male friend (yeah, my Sugar Daddy...who else?) with me through the whole event. He even took time off from his work to take care of me in his house while I was recovering. Before my operation, I told him I didn't think I would need his caregiver services and I would be able to take care of myself in my apartment. Boy was I wrong and boy was I glad he stuck to his guns insisting I let him take care of me. When I woke up from surgery, I was dizzy, thirsty, and I had this very tight wrap around my new boobs. I wasn't in pain then because I was still under the effect of the anesthetic...but the pain came latter...lots of pain...lots and lots of pain. Fuck.

My friend installed me on a couch in the sitting room of his bedroom. I say installed, because he had to position me at a 45 degree angle against an arm on his couch and pack pillows all around me. We tried his bed first...but it just hurt too much. He kept me well drugged on Oxycontin the first night, only getting me up to go to the bathroom and to clean and rewrap my boobs (I know you're saying what a tough job he had...but it was, I was in pain and a bitch the whole time). The next day we drove about 30 miles over bumpy roads for a follow up check with my doctor. I felt every one of those fucking bumps. After that, I stayed three more days on my friend's couch with him nursing me, to include not only giving me more medicine, but also doing more cleaning and bandaging, giving me sponge baths, and combing my hair. He even had to pull my panties down and back up after I peed. Very humiliating, but I couldn't do it myself. I was a total medical wreck and he was a total saint. I will never forget him for doing that. We had only one bad experience. He was trying to re-tuck me into my pillow nest after going to the bathroom and he accidentally bumped one of my boobs. Oh the pain...and the bad words that came out of my mouth. I felt bad about cussing him, he felt even worse about hurting me. But we got over it. I was back to dancing the next week with my swollen, shiny, brand new boobs. Yes, they were very shiny because my skin was stretched very tightly over an expanded area. I still believe having them done was the best investment I've ever made.

One more thing and again, I don't know how to put this politely. As a nude dancer, you just have to have a good looking punani. I've seen a lot of ugly punanis on beautiful women, with their inner labia dangling way beyond their outer labia. That is just plain unattractive, it looks like they have dog-chewed clams between their legs. I can imagine being a customer watching these girls dance. They look great in their costumers and by all appearances they have very sexy bodies...until they take their g-string off. Then it's like "Oh My God." And to make matters worse, some of these girls have piercings running through these extended lips calling even more attention to how stretched out they are….Ubangi pussies….Ha Ha. I think at this point, their customers decide to move elsewhere. I don't have any hangy down parts,,,,yet, thank God. If I did, I would seriously consider having surgery to fix the problem which I've heard is pretty minor. If you think I'm a little overboard with this advice, wait until I tell you later about applying make up to your punani. If you are a nude dancer, there is no such thing as being too personal considering how closely you will be scrutinized by every customer you see.

- Costumes

I know, I know… we're nude dancers so you're probably asking why we need to worry about a costume that's only on our bodies for a short time with each customer. The answer – why do fishermen put bait on their hooks? Enticement. We have to first lure customers out of the crowd before we can start getting our garters stuffed with dollar bills. This means wearing sexy costumes to get their attention and stimulate their libidos and fantasies. Picking the right costume is not as easy as you think because there's a fine line between showing too much and not showing enough. You want to tantalize but not reveal. You also have to consider what color looks best on you, glitter or no glitter, costume theme, etc. Theme? Remember I talked about the Nun's outfit earlier? Little schoolgirl outfits are always <u>very</u> popular, perverted…no…very perverted…but popular. Naughty nurse costumes are also a hit with our customers. I've never seen a Little Bo Peep costume with sheep…and I don't think I want to. I really wouldn't want to have a customer who is there for the sheep and not the dancer. That brings up a whole new niche market which I think is really small, not many shepherds in the U.S. any more. Ha Ha. Now ladies, don't get all holier than thou with this. Isn't the stereotypical male dancer always dressed as a construction worker or a fireman or policeman? I think women may be more into role playing then men. Men just want to see naked women and want whatever costume we're wearing laying on the dance floor at our feet just as quickly as possible.

I'm not into themes for some reason, never have been. What I like to wear is a very small g-string covered by a tight pair of booty shorts or panties, topped off with a colorful, tight bra that showcases my boobs. Why do I wear two pairs of pants?…DUH. The more clothes I have on, the more it will cost the customer to have me take them off. **And they don't come off with the first two or three dollars a customer stuffs into my garter.** I'll talk more about garter management strategies later. Speaking of costumes, I wonder what strippers wear in Muslim countries? It would cost a customer a fortune to get a dancer out of all the layers of clothes they traditionally wear. And really, the whole thing might come down to one unpleasant surprise. Just imagine a customer sitting down to a girl dancing in a full-body burkha with several layers of underclothing. He doesn't know whether or not the girl he's watching dance is attractive or ugly or what kind of a body she has. And he won't know until she finally takes her clothes off. Ha Ha. I think it would be like a little boy unwrapping a Christmas present expecting a great toy to play with only to find a pair of sox or underwear. Sorry…just a little offensive stripper humor, I've been around too many of the military here in Hawaii. I'm sure an Imam is already writing a Fatwa on my ass. But it's all conjecture anyway since they don't have any strippers, not even in paradise where the only women they're supposed to meet are virgins. Of course I don't think anyone has ever defined whether these virgins are male or female. Surprise Achmet!! Ha Ha. Besides why are they so obsessed with virgins when a young guy would have a much better time with a bevy of sexually uninhibited experienced women? Ha Ha. For a guy, I would think a better paradise would be 72 beautiful hookers who think you're a millionaire. Ha Ha. And oh, by the way, they like to work in groups….anyone for a ménage à trois? Or a ménage à quartre? Or ménage à cinq? Ha Ha...I've known some guys who wouldn't settle for anything less than a ménage à vingt (look it up yourself). Ha Ha

Anyway, getting back to the costumes we wear in the Hot Zone, I like colors that best show off my brown skin, and I like my panties tight. If I show a little camel toe, great! That's just frosting on the cake…. bait for the trap…a trailer for an epic movie. Ha Ha. I'm firmly convinced dancers, and women in general, are much sexier in suggestive clothing than naked. For me, having a

few skimpy clothes on allows the customer's imagination, fueled by his horniness, to run wild. If all goes well, he's got a diamond cutter-hard on before I even start taking my clothes off and at that point, his little brain is in total control of his wallet and common sense and the dollar bills are flying into my garter. Of course, we dancers refuse to advantage of a customer in this unstable mental condition…. NOT…ARE YOU STUPID?…we try very hard to get our customers into this in that condition. It's our primary business plan (this is my college degree talking). Little brain dominance is how we convince customers to take us to the Table Dance room or the Private Dance room upstairs. At some point in the alcohol and sperm overload, spending a lot of money in one of these private dancing areas just seems to makes a lot of financial sense to the customer. Ha Ha. Remember what I said about sexiness? If you can see a little wet spot on the front of a customer's pants, pre-cum from his dick, then you've got him by the balls. Mentally, he's lying in bed making wild monkey love to you while you're dancing. A little whisper in his ear, soft caresses on his shoulders and arms just add fuel to the already raging fire. And I continually add fuel to the fire, all the while pulling my garter away from my leg with a quick, money making, rhythm that would make any rap star proud. Just listen to the syncopated rhythm of the garter belt boogie…snap…snap…..
snap…snap…snap…money in the bank….bank…...bank....!

- Shoes

I could have included a discussion of shoes while talking about costumes above; however, I couldn't really find a proper point do that without ruining the flow of my thoughts on the other costume parts. So here we are. Don't get me wrong, I think a good pair of shoes is very important to the overall impression a dancer makes, if I didn't I wouldn't discuss them at all. You cannot just wear a pair of slippers or street shoes as part of your costume. After all, you've invested a lot of money into buying an attention grabbing costume that will lure in customers so you do you want to blow that look by wearing an ugly pair of shoes. NO!!! If you read Penthouse, shoes are a very significant fetish for a lot of men. My current boyfriend insists I wear high heels when we have sex. Why? Because a really good pair high heels lifts your butt up very enticingly...or should I say invitingly. After all isn't that why high heels were invented, to make a woman's butt more prominent and inviting? And ask Sir Mix-A-Lot if he likes butts...."*Baby Got Back*"...oh yea!!! And who invented high heels? A man of course! DUH!! Anyhow, having my butt stick out is great for me because it's one of my best features. If I were to fill out a resume as a dancer, I would put my butt down as one of my strong points. And the heels only make it better.

Being in Hawaii with a lot of Asian girls who are generally shorter than their Caucasian counterparts, you will see a lot of very high platform shoes on dancers. I have high shoes because I am also short, but I don't go to the heights some of these girls do. I've seen some shoes that practically require a step ladder to strap on.

Of course, having these high heels can get dangerous. Dancers can fall off their shoes and break their ankles or fall off the stage. I've seen shoes with live goldfish in the heels or that light up when you walk. I'm a little more conservative in my shoe choice. I want my shoes to work hand in hand with my costume, not call attention away from it. I like all white or black shoes, clear shoes, and shoes that sparkle. I don't need a tall pair of shoes to make me look taller; I have my ego for that...Ha Ha. Besides as I tell my boyfriends, there's no such thing as a girl being too short in bed.

One last point, heels are very good in a fight which can be very handy when you work in a strip club. They're also great when you want to immediately correct the ill-advised actions of some perverted customer or fellow dancer. I can just imagine the reaction of an emergency room doctor looking at my heel buried in the brain of a rude strip club customer. Ha Ha. Cause of death: Fatal stripper-heel-induced brain trauma. Not something you'd record in an obituary of a prominent businessman. And of course, it would be justifiable homicide or the mid-course correction of a stray Darwinian DNA strand that doesn't need to propagate further into the general gene pool population.

- *Makeup*

Artfully applied makeup is a time consuming but necessary preparation all dancers have to go through before they report into work, and periodically, while they're working. Most women spend a lot of time applying makeup just in the course of their daily routine before they go to work, shopping, or out on a date. Dancers have to be a little more meticulous; some even have their makeup professionally applied. In essence, we're selling ourselves and we have to look beautiful under harsh lighting and close customer scrutiny. Any blemish will stand out like a neon sign. It's a pretty simple equation, if we're unappealing, we won't get any customers and we'll go home with no money. Even us non-math majors understand this. We can't even compensate for having done a poor makeup job by wearing beautiful clothes...because....everyone chime in on the chorus....WE'RE NAKED MOST OF THE TIME. For this very reason, we also can't stop applying makeup at the bottom of the neck; it's actually a whole body experience to include out boobs and punani. And yes, I know you perverts are going to ask - even my other nether orifice...I said the whole body...HA HA. Why the punani? Because most exotic dancers shave them! Our punanis are the centerpiece of our dancing so they need to be shown in all their glory, not hidden under a mound of pubic hair. Our customers expect (and want) to see a new born (or even more perverted) little girl look – read no hair. They want an up close, unobstructed view. Since we can't hide them they're by God going to have makeup applied to them. Believe it or not, the naked crotch is just not that attractive. Mine's a little darker than the rest of my skin for some reason; it's even worse if I haven't shaved recently (like right before I go to work) and it has a little stubble. So I apply a light tan makeup...caramel color if you're really curious. I know my customers probably wouldn't care if my punani looked a little dark, most are not that discerning, all they want to see is pussy. But I care; it's the professional in me. I want to look my best at all times….all of me, and as I said earlier that includes the place where the sun doesn't shine, it gets a swipe of makeup too.

After years of shaving, I have to admit I like being bare. It's certainly much cleaner, especially if you have a gentleman guest munching away down there Ha Ha. A couple of months ago, I did a small survey of my customers as part of the research for this book. I asked them if they like a lot of pubic hair, a little hair, or no hair. It was pretty much unanimous, no hair…period. As I said earlier, they all liked that "little girl" look, the perverts. And I'm just as perverted by catering to their pedophile fantasies. It's not just dancers who effect the "little girl" look. Ladies, look at yourselves, how much pubic hair do you have - none or just a very little? Why? You're not dancers trying to please customers. Oh, you do it for you man? Well then, you're catering to his pedophile fantasies. Ha Ha. You might as well face it ladies, the days of having pubic hair, or a lot of pubic hair, are gone for everyone. Go to any beach and you'll see women in thongs so small they might as well be dancing in the Hot Zone because they're showing their ass and punani anyway. There's just no room for even a stray strand of pubic hair; it makes for great camel toes....Ha Ha.

Lastly, before we stop talking about makeup, I want to briefly mention one other makeup touch I really like - sparkles. Some nights I put sparkles all over my body…I think that an extra little touch that really draws in the customers because a sparkling naked body really sexy under the lights on the stage. Draws in all those customers with Tinker Bell fantasies…Ha Ha. The only problem with sparkles; however, is they're damn hard to get off your body; it can take several showers to wash them away, and even then, you'll find a few in all your nooks and crannies. They also get all over your furniture and carpet. I've had some customers actually refuse to let me give them a lap dance when I work bachelor parties with sparkles on. They don't want to go home after the party and explain the sparkles on their clothes to their significant others. Ladies, if you're going nightclubbing, you might want to be a little naughty and put just a small touch of sparkles just at the top of your boobs, maybe elsewhere on your body too if you are expecting to be really naughty. Ha Ha.

- Hair

I think well groomed, good smelling hair is a turn on for a customer that many dancers neglect take advantage of. I don't care if it's long or short, but a dancer's overall appearance will be hurt if her hair is dirty and uncombed. To most women, taking care of their hair is like breathing, a skill they've honed since childhood under their Mother's or Grandmother's gentle guidance. Women spend fortunes in beauty parlors to get their hair just right. But I've seen dancers who obviously missed this lesson and thereby look unappealing no matter how good their dancing costume is or how good they otherwise look naked. I'm not addressing any particular style of hair style, in fact I'm fine with all types just as long as they're well groomed. I like mine long, straight, and dark brown with only a hint of streaking. My hair is a tool I use when I dance. I often drape it over a customer's head or dangle it over his crotch. It's one of the few parts of my body I can touch a customer with and not get reprimanded, so it has to be clean and fragrant.

One last thing - hair color. I know now days you can color your hair any shade invented by God, and I see women on the street and in the Hot Zone taking advantage of that freedom by sporting a lot of difference colors, some bordering on the bizarre. I've seen some colors I wish I hadn't assaulted my eyes with. I guess I'm getting conservative in my old age, but I think dancers who wear a wild colored hair, such as bright yellow or purple, actually hurt their business. Like tattoos or piercings, a wild hair color may appeal to a small niche of customer types but if you're in business to make as much money as possible you want to appeal to the widest audience as possible and not limited yourself to just a small niche of customers. To me, this means keep your hair color and streaking conservative. Although I'm Filipino with naturally black hair, I do like to color my hair a dark brown color with a little light streaking. You will never see fluorescent orange streaks or tips. This is just my opinion though, and in the end ladies, you're welcome to die your hair whatever freakin' color you want. You can even dye your pubic hair green with yellow stripes. It's a free country afterall. And your customers will likewise feel the same freedom to spend money on dancers they feel most attracted to…like conservative me for instance.

- Perfume

One of the bottom line accessories for any dancer is a good perfume. You can have the most beautiful face and body in the world, and wear the best costumes, but if you stink, it's sayonara to any customers. YOU HAVE TO SMELL GOOD. I know I told you men are primarily visual creatures, and for the most part they are, but I can't tell you how many customers have told me how good I smell. A little earlier, I talked about how good smelling hair is a customer turn on. Likewise, the rest of your body has to smell just as good and inviting because that's sometimes the deal maker in enticing a customer to linger and continue depositing money into your garter belt. I had one customer tell me that when I come close to him, he closed his eyes and fantasized off the nearness of my body and my perfume. You don't have to use an expensive perfume, and believe me some of them can be expensive. The smell just has to fit you and work well with your body chemistry. I've always liked Victoria's Secret. It's not expensive and it comes in a variety of scents which I use every night depending on my mood. I just think it's very intimate smelling and I get a lot of customer compliments, particularly for the Peaches and Cream scent. I can't think of a better endorsement of my choice of perfume than a customer taking a deep whiff every time I get close to him and then telling me I smell great. When you smell good and you know it, you're at your highest level of confidence. Unfortunately, if you smell sweaty or use some strong smelling cheap perfume you'll also know it because you'll get immediate feedback from customers who leave in a hurry or by the empty chair in front of you that no one wants to sit in. You don't have to apply a lot; in fact, a little restraint is best. You want just enough to give a customer gets a very gentle whiff of a pleasant fragrance whenever he comes near you. With perfume, less definitely equals more. Smelling good is something I work on constantly when I dance because it's very easy to sweat when the club is crowded and warm. I constantly take small breaks to freshen up by reapplying my perfume.

Last but not least, if you're a nude dancer you have to smell extremely good between your legs, especially in Hawaii where customers can get really get an up close and personal gynecological view of your punani. Some of my customers have their noses no more than a fraction of an inch from mine. Do you think he'd be there if I didn't smell "flower fresh"? I should have said flower fresh and edible....Ha Ha. I don't want my punani to smell like fish and taste like chicken, as the joke goes. Well, maybe tasting like chicken isn't all that bad. Ha Ha.

- Tattoos

I guess it's a sign of the times that more and more women now have tattoos - Body Art. Tattoos used to be primarily a male adornment for gangsters, sailors, and other lowlifes. Sometimes women had them too – hookers and strippers, but these were generally were small and unobtrusive. Good girls never had one. No women had them in the Philippines when I was growing up. It just wasn't done. Now, maybe as a product of the hip-hop generation, more women have them than don't; and they can be just as large and as nasty as those on the men. As I look around the club, there are a lot of tattoos on the dancers; most are sporting more than one tattoo. I've seen tattoos in every imaginable place on both the dancers and the customers. Some are huge. One of my fellow dancers has a dragon that covers her back with its tail wrapping completely around her body and the head near her belly button. Another dancer has two six guns, one on either side of her belly button with the barrel extending down into her pants. Guess where the barrels end up? Several dancers have complex tattoos that are bordering on a complete body suit. Me? I finally bowed to the temptation and peer pressure and got a small one on my shoulder a couple years ago. It's not intrusive to my overall appearance by any means and can easily be covered when convention calls for it. I was ambivalent about getting it until the end. The problem with tattoos is they can sometimes limit your appeal to customers. I'm all business, remember? It really boils down to a customer's personal taste of how he wants his fantasy girl to look. With tattoos, it might be a 50/50 toss up as to whether or not it will appeal to the majority of customers. I think the odds for a customer liking a dancer with tattoos drop dramatically the more tattoos the dancer has. Fortunately (or unfortunately), whatever your views on the subject are, as I said earlier, almost all women now have tattoos. This has gone a long way in reducing the negativity. Even the most virginal, "girl-next-door" women now have a small tattoo somewhere. Now the issue pretty much boils down to what the tattoos are and how many, with a dancer being literally covered from head to toe in tattoos still being pretty much viewed negatively, at least by me. Would I let my daughter get one? Would you? I think the vote is still out on that. But I think it would be very hard for me to tell my daughter no you can't have one, when I have one on my shoulder.

- Piercings

Piercings are another fad I've seen increase in popularity over the last couple of years. I don't mean just earrings. Like tattoos, I've seen piercings everywhere on both dancers and customers, some of which must have been agonizing to put into place. I'm talking nipple and clit rings on the women and on the men? One guy showed me right there in the club a half dozen rings piercing his penis, both through the foreskin and through the "fireman's hat" for crying out loud. I'm a women and just thinking about that makes me cringe. I'm betting there was a lot of alcohol or drugs involved. Quite a few girls have belly button piercings with a small pendant extending down for about three inches below the belly button. Depending on the pendant, I think they look good, but you need to have a really flat stomach for them, something I have trouble with. I don't think I'll be getting one soon even though I've had customers offer to pay for it. I can't even imagine getting either a nipple or clit ring; I don't like pain, especially in those sensitive areas. What if you snag your blouse or bra on the nipple ring and tear it out? Kind of like guys snagging their dicks in their pant zipper. The dancers that have a clit ring say it enhances their sexual experiences, especially the ring that has a little ball that sits right in front of the clit. All I can say to that is "You go Girl!!" ....but NOT FOR ME!! I think it's fun to watch men when a girl first exposes the clit ring to them. Being sexually aroused is not a term I would use to describe their first reactions. Most seem to mentally cover up their groins and I can see the gears turning in their minds, "How would it feel for my member to be sliding past that? How would it feel if my member got snagged on that ring?" Not very positive impressions....Ha Ha.

As with tattoos, piercings can impact dramatically how a customer views a dancer and influence his decision of whether or not to have her dance for him. In moderation, the presence of a piercing (one or two at most) may not have any impact on the customer; some may even be turned on by a modest belly button ring or even a clit ring. But call me old fashion; I strongly think that a girl who sports a body full of piercings will only appeal to a minority of the customers that come into the Hot Zone. In other words, the dancers here with a number of piercings are limiting their customer base unnecessarily, which I can't understand, me being the bottom line person that I am. How many piercings do I have? Just my earrings. Like I said, I've thought about a belly button piercing from time to time but haven't given into the temptation. I certainly won't until I lose a little weight on my stomach, which may boil down to NEVER. I most certainly will NEVER get nipple rings or God forbid a clit ring; I cringe at just thinking about them.

The Ladies

I've reached the point in my ramblings where it might be interesting to describe the different types of dancers I've worked with. I'm also going to do quick descriptions of some of the rules and customs (official and unofficial) that govern conduct between these dancers and their relationship with customers. As I talk about the dancers, I'm not going to mention names for obvious reasons, just general types. I'll do the same thing later with the customers I've see. My goal is to give you a behind the scenes look at inside the stripping profession from the perspective of a dancer......me. I think you'll find it enlightening, certainly interesting, and in the case of the customers, a little disturbing.

- *The Beginner.*

All dancers, including me, were beginners at one time. We all walked into a strip club for the first time wearing a skimpy outfit and our best smile, and all violently shaking from fright. We had two career options at that point, overcome our fear or walk the hell back out the door and quit. Beginners are not hard to spot or sympathize with; they have the same look Christians did as they were thrown to the lions during the time of Nero. You want to chuckle to yourself when you see them, but you also <u>have to</u> give them the respect they're due. The fact they're on stage means they've overcome significant personal hurdles to even get to this point. One of the biggest hurdles being nude dancing in front of strangers goes against everything they've ever been taught by their parents about modesty and socially acceptable behavior. Stripping contravenes all these conventions. Perversely, they also worry how these same strangers <u>will like</u> their body. They wonder how they will (or should) react if the body they're proud of is rejected as ugly and no one wants to watch them dance. That said, it's no wonder beginners look very uncomfortable (or charitably, uncertain) with a "what the hell am I doing here" look on their face (some call it a "deer in the headlights" look). It also doesn't help that they're usually the youngest girls on the stage. They move awkwardly and watch the more experienced dancers next to them to learn dance moves and, importantly, how to relate to the customers sitting in front of them. Shyness is sometimes a big contributor to this awkwardness. Most new dancers have never been naked for anyone except their boyfriends and even that bareness was probably lessened somewhat by a blanket or by keeping the room dark. It isn't unusual for a beginner to hesitate taking off all her clothes, the bottoms being the hardest of all to remove. I've seen some beginners really struggle to give a customer a little peek of anything. It says a lot about the girl's morality (maybe that's why my clothes just flew off the first time…Ha Ha), but it doesn't do much for their career as a stripper. Eventually, if she doesn't get over this shyness, customers will stop asking her to dance and she'll have to make the decision to get naked or go home. Most eventually cave and begin actually stripping. I think that's sad in a way, another girl compromised, but it's the nature of the business.

If the beginners are lucky, one of the more experienced dancers will take them under their wing and teach them enough skills to survive and profit. I've never been that generous, you don't show your competition how to be better at taking customers from you. STUPID! One thing I hate to see; however, and something I have lectured new girls on, is not to give their nakedness away. Beginners, and sometimes even experienced dancers, seem shy about pulling their garter as a hint for the customer to deposit more money into the meter. Instead, they'll take their clothes off as fast as they can and hope the customer will at least put a little money in their garter. THAT'S NOT THE WAY TO DO IT! The Rule of Thumb I've always lived by and what I tell these new dancers: Don't ever get naked right away...and don't give it away cheaply when you do! You have something a customer wants to see very badly - your punani. It's the law of supply and demand, you have something he wants so make him pay well for the privilege because once he sees it, he'll probably get up and move on to another girl unless you've also hit him with the sexual attitude whammy or get him talking to you (remember my earlier discussion of job skills?). I would say that out of $20 dollars, I'll begin to give a customer a peek under my bra at the $5 dollar point, keeping my booty shorts with the g-string under them chastely intact. At $10, I'll take my bra off and begin pulling my shorts and g-string aside for a brief glimpse of my punani. This is just a brief glimpse, because I want him whipping out more money for more peeks, hoping eventually that I'll finally shed both to give him the full Monty. At $15, my shorts are off, and I'm dancing just in my g-string. This time I'll pull the g-string aside to give him longer peeks and from different perspectives such as my legs spread in front of him or giving him a rear view while I'm on my hands and knees…. but the g-string still remains on my body. By then the little brain in his pants is driving him mercilessly, forcing him to open his wallet up; he's totally invested at this point so he can't quit before he sees the good stuff - me being buck ass naked. At $20, I may have the g-string pulled down to my knees briefly as a tease before pulling it back up again to resume the side of the panties curtain shows. I usually don't like to get completely naked, but I will on occasion if a customer has been very generous ($40+). Men, if you got me totally naked, feel privileged. I get really angry when I see a new girl taking off her g-string with only $2 or $3 dollars in her garter. This is bad for her and bad for me if I'm dancing next to her. Why? What customer would be willing to invest $20 or more to see my punani when the girl next to me is giving it away for next to nothing? It gives stripping a bad name, and even worse, cuts down on my income. You see, despite my efforts to look cool in this book, I can be emotionally invested at times, especially if my livelihood is threatened. So stand back!!!

- The Old Pro

I guess this is my category unfortunately. I hate the word "old" in any connotation…how about just "The Pros?" as the title to this section? The pros are the "been – there, done – that", dancers, each having seen it all and done it all, sometimes literally.

For the customers this means they'll either get a dancer who's expert at sexually titillating them and giving them a memorable experience, or they'll get the stereotypical "harden" stripper, chewing vigorously on a piece of gum, going through the motions of stripping with mechanical efficiency and a disassociated thousand yard stare. If they have any professional pride at all, these experienced dancers will work at <u>not</u> looking like hardened strippers or <u>not</u> looking totally disgusted with humanity or men in general to give that good performance for their customers. In other words, they'll be great actresses. They'll also have to fight hard not to turn their routines into an impersonal, assembly line stripping act, working through one customer after another as quickly as possible. Customers will quickly sense this indifference if not from their first look at the dancer, then very quickly after they sit down in front of her and she starts pulling her garter belt out in a rhythm quick enough to make a rap artist envious. A harden pro can squeeze $20 out of a customer before he can even get two sips of his drink at which point the customer will (and probably should) get up quickly and walk away before he goes broke in the first ten minutes he's in the club.

I can't bad mouth all old pro dancers however, probably because I'm one... Ha Ha. Impersonal or not, one thing a customer will get is a professional. The Pro will exercise constantly to keep her body in excellent shape, she'll take pride in her stripping outfits, and she won't be afraid to show the sexuality the customer is there to see, within the limit of the law of course. They are also not afraid to work the system as I do occasionally when I'm with a customer I like and I want him to keep coming back. As with all of these girls, I have a list of steady customers who come into the club just to see me. In fact, they have my phone number and will call or text to see if I'm working on a particular night. For some, I will come into the club even if I had intended to take the night off just because they're good customers and good spenders. It's not good business to say no to them and then having them move their patronage to some other dancers

Although I admit I'm an old pro, I don't gouge customers for as much money as I can in the shortest time possible. In fact I take pride in that. Well, maybe I do for assholes and perverts, then no mercy. The trick is to screw them and not have them realize they're being screwed until they look down and find empty wallets. Ha Ha. I take great pains to individually engage each and every customer who sits down in front of me (remember we talked about talking and listening earlier?) because I strongly believe that's the key to getting a customer to stay and keep spending, especially if they're lonely and most are. I'm happy to report there are more pros like me than the other kind, the impersonal hardened stripper. But you'll run across these hardened strippers in every club, so it's buyer beware. I also find some of the older pro's hard to work with especially if they're nearing the end of their shelf life and have to struggle for customers. There are times when the club is busy and we'll refer customers to another dancer or we'll share a customer with a dancer if he wants a two'fer. Dancing is much more fun when everyone is laughing and cooperating with each other. But there are some girls you just can't do that with, and it's usually the harden pro. They're there to make their own money and everyone else can go to hell. There will be no frivolity with the other dancers. They don't interact or talk with the other dancers, they just dance. And when they're done, they go home. Please God don't ever make me like that.

The Pro dancers are exactly the girls who should be thinking about their future after stripping. Some do, and work on college degrees for future careers while they dance. In the Hot Zone, we have one girl who just finished a Master's Degree in Nursing and wants to be a nursing teacher. Why she's still stripping I don't know. I asked her once and didn't get a very good answer. Maybe she doesn't know or just wants to squeeze out that last little bit of her shelf life before she moves on. Making a lot of easy money can be addictive and hard to step away from even if you have a good education. I have another fellow dancer who has a BA degree in Finance from the University of Texas. Yet, she's still dancing, or maybe I should just say "and yet, she's a dancer", because I haven't a clue why she even started dancing with her education. As I said earlier, I just received a Bachelor of Science degree, in Information Systems no less. Yah, I'm a Nerd. Will I keep stripping now that I have my degree? Good question. I want to say no, but economics are economics so I'll probably hang on for a little while until I can get THE job that will comfortably allow me to support my mother and keep a roof over our heads.

And when I finally make that leap to an acceptable professional career outside of dancing, my dance clothes will go into an incinerator with the appropriate religious incantations and ceremony to ensure my stripping life will become just a distant memory. Well maybe I won't burn my clothes. I've done the "burn and celebrate" act too many times in the past when I thought I finally had THE job or the PERSONAL RELATIONSHIP (husband/boyfriend) that would get me out of stripping only to have to buy more dancing outfits when my WAY OUT failed. FUCK. Wait a minute, let me walk outside and scream this from the street corner….FUCK!!!

- *The Acrobats*

The Hot Zone features a vertical brass "stripper" pole at all four corners of their stages with each pole connected to one another at the top by a horizontal pole about seven feet up. In essence, each stage is an enclosed cage defined by the poles. Most of the dancers will use the vertical poles occasionally to maintain their balance as they lift their legs to give customers a better view of their punani. I rarely use these poles because I don't like to stand when I'm naked, preferring the better privacy offered by just sitting in front of my customer. There are some dancers; however, that use both the vertical and horizontal poles vigorously when they perform. In a way, some of these girls are really the stereotypes people have in mind when they think of strippers….i.e. dancing around a stripper pole. Other dancers take great delight in swinging around the poles like they're kids on a playground jungle gym. God love 'em. I call them the acrobats and I tip my hat to each and every one of them for expending more energy in a single dance than I do an entire night. You can see them every night swinging with abandon from the high horizontal poles and shimmying up and down the vertical poles, clothed and unclothed, with the agility of monkeys. Some don't slow down long enough to let customers put money their garter, so I'm not sure if they're dancing to make money or just for the fun of it. But they are something to behold, particularly as they hang up-side-down from the vertical poles with only their leg strength keeping them from doing a face plant on the stage. I sometimes have visions of them slipping off the horizontal poles as they swing and flying out into the crowd surrounding the stage. I have one friend in particular, an Indian (from India in case you're wondering), who takes great joy in swinging around on the poles. But she is young and stupid, she'll learn. She has a strong Indian ethnical appearance which does not attract many customers so I think her pole antics are her way of attracting customers that wouldn't otherwise give her a second look. If that works, more power to her, but the pole just isn't for me. I'd probably kill myself on the damn thing. Chances are the poles will be the death of me anyway when one of the pole monkeys slips and lands on little me.

- *The Superstars*

I probably should have talked about these dancers first but I don't particularly like them, so here we are right after the acrobats. Every strip club has one or two superstars. They are the dancers you see in the advertisements for the clubs, the headliners who always have a customer in front of them and other customers lined up to be next for the pleasure of watching her dance. They're the girls the club staff treats with kid gloves, no admonishments or hassles. They're the most beautiful dancers in a club full of beautiful dancers. Get the idea? You think I'm jealous? I can say with all honesty, I'm not. In fact, I think I'm a beneficiary of their drawing power. The club gets more customers as a whole because of these well-publicized superstars and more customers means better business for me, so I see no need for jealousy. Of course there are superstars and there are superstars. A superstar in one of the lower class clubs is not as beautiful as one in an upper class club; she just has fewer physical flaws then the dancers around her. But who cares, in her own environment she's the most popular girl around, the queen within the confines of her club.

Speaking of superstars, I have to wonder how many keep dancing well past their shelf lives because they liked being in the spotlight and stupidly thought it would never end. Consequently, they never developed an exit strategy and now suddenly find themselves unwanted, used-up dancers. I call them the over-the-hill dancers and I'll discuss them later.

- The Not Quite So Pretty Girls

These are the dancers that break your heart. They're not as attractive as the majority of the girls in the club and have to struggle to make money. They're ignored when every other dancer is overwhelmed with customers. This leaves them resorting to wandering around the club trying unsuccessfully to get customers to buy them a Lady's drink or a private dance. Why do I feel sorry for them? Maybe it's because I know how hard they struggle and see how rude customers can be to them. It doesn't matter if these dancers are the nicest people in the world, they're fighting an uphill battle trying and failing in a beauty-dictated work environment. Often a club owner will get tired of them occupying his dance stage with little return on investment and tell them not to come back. A lot of the girls in the Hot Zone get an appearance fee for just showing up and staying at least six hours (remember we're independent contractors). Many of the marginal dancers don't get this money because the club owner is trying to discourage them. Although I've never done it, I sometimes want to advise these girls to try a less classier club, like the one I started with. They won't be competing with dancers better looking than they are, so their chances of making money are better, they may even be the prettiest girl in the club. The catch is they may have to lower their moral standards a little. But that's totally up to them until the choice is eventually taken out of their hands when the Hot Zone owner tells them thank you for working here but please don't come back. Then their choices are the lower class club or "Would you like french fries with that order?"

- *The Bitches*

There are always dancers in every club that just can't get along with anyone for various reasons or no reason at all. You can tell what I think of these dancers by the name of this section –

Bitches. If this were a school situation, they would be the schoolyard bullies beating up smaller or more timid children and taking their lunch money. They also tend to have a "posse" of strap hangers who know they're weak and vulnerable on their own so they attached themselves to the strongest person they can find. Your first thought may be these are the ugliest girls in the club and jealously is driving their aggression. That's the case sometimes, but not always. Some women are just bitches...period. They can be attractive and still be bitches. Whatever the reason, we have to work with them, or work around them, which is a pain. It's especially a pain if they've decided to pick on you for whatever reason. I told you earlier, I was the target of two Bitches, one in each of the clubs I worked in. I don't know if it is coincidence, but both were heavily tattooed local girls (Samoan) and both mean and aggressive. I don't know what it is about me; I mind my own business and don't engage on any level with most of my fellow dancers. Sometimes dancers can get a little territorial, and the ones that have to struggle to get customers a little more so. That was probably the reason for me running afoul of the Bitch in my first club. The other Bitch I ran into was here in the Hot Zone. She took a disliking to me right after I first got here. Like the first, she seemed to take umbrage at my existence and would point at me and call me names. I honest to God don't know why she decided to pick on me, unless, as I speculated for the first girl, this second Bitch thought I was cutting in on her territory. Anyway, I didn't get beat up this time and she was eventually fired, probably for having a bad attitude I'm thinking. But for several months thereafter, I walked out to my car in the club parking lot constantly looking over my shoulder thinking this girl would blame me for being fired and would try to beat me up. As an aside, I was in my neighborhood grocery store the other day looking at the meat counter. While I was there, a man walked over and stood next to me also looking at the meat selections. Although we never said a word to each other, his wife/girlfriend practically ran over and physically inserted herself between me and the guy, bumping me in the process. I got a face full of stink eye from her before she dragged her husband/boyfriend off. Again, I absolutely did nothing to incite any jealous reaction like that from this girl. All I could think of is "Damn, it's hard to be beautiful and have a great body." Ha Ha. Maybe that's the real reason I'm the target of the Bitches...I'm Hot. Yeah...as if. Ha Ha.

- The "Why the Hell Are They Dancing" Girls

Some girls truly make me scratch my head regarding their reasons for dancing or continuing to dance. I'm talking about girls with college degrees or girls with either a husband or boyfriend (or both Ha Ha). I've already told you about two of my fellow dancers who have advanced college degrees and yet still dance, one of them even receives money from a substantial trust fund. So, what the fuck? In these instances, I can probably say it's the thrill of dancing or exhibitionism that keeps them around. Or maybe they are still looking for Mr. Right. If so, I can tell them right now, a strip club is no place to meet Mr. Right, every customer we see here has substantial flaws in their personalities. That leaves the dancers with boyfriends and husbands. Why are they still dancing? I can probably understand dancing even when you have a boyfriend because boyfriends are so temporary and the romance can be over as quickly as it started leaving you with nothing. But what about those girls with husbands? Do they want luxuries that their husbands are unwilling or unable to provide? Or are we talking about thrill seeking and exhibitionism again? My other thought is their marriage isn't really all that solid and these girls are also looking for a Mr. Right to replace their husbands.

The irony of this whole section, or rather me offering any type of advice or critical observations in this section is I kept dancing in my first job even though I had a husband; in fact he was a rich husband. And if you're not already tired of me bragging about it, I also now have a college degree. So, a basic question to me is, why the fuck AM I still dancing? With 20/20 hindsight I can tell you that it was a big mistake for me to continue dancing after I got married to my second husband. I wanted some luxuries and was afraid to ask for them even though I knew he could afford them. You saw how well that turned out – exit husband number two. I'm still dancing now even with a degree because I haven't yet gotten THE job that will allow me to quit and keep fully supporting myself and my mother. It's that whole eating and having shelter thing that's hard to maintain in expensive Hawaii. But I can assure you in all honesty, when I do find THAT job, the door of the Hot

Zone will not hit me in the ass on my way out. Like the Roadrunner, it'll be Beep Beep and I'm gone!!!!

- The Waiting for Mr. Right Girls

I've pounded the dais a number of times with the theme that all dancers need to have an exit strategy, a Plan B to call into play when their dancing life is over. Some don't and often end up dancing until the club owner tells them they're no longer needed because no customer wants to see them naked. My plan B was to get a degree (which I've done) and find a job, a career actually, that will allow me to quit stripping on my own terms (still in work). You'll notice I haven't considered the possibility of having a husband in my Plan B...been there and done that with lousy results. So if I come up with another husband, one that's a keeper, it'll be a pleasant surprise and a bonus, but the lack of one won't hurt my after-stripping career plans. For other dancers, if they bother to have a Plan B at all, it's just to meet a Mr. Right who'll marry them and take them out of the dancing life (on a white horse no less). As the years go by and they find themselves still dancing, their criterion for Mr. Right slowly downgrades from Mr. Right to a Mr. "He'll Do" to even Mr. "What the Hell, He's a Man and He's Got Money". Marriage is usually the immediate goal because even if it fails, the ex-dancer can live off the alimony. If there is no marriage, the girl might find herself back dancing and looking for another Mr. Right. I know several dancers who did meet Mr. Right and married him, only to return to dancing because Mr. Right couldn't afford to pay the bills or needed money to buy drugs. Sad. Sadder still are those girls who never meet Mr. Right, or a facsimile thereof, and don't have a Plan C to progress to. These are the dancers we're going to discuss next, the "Over-the-Hill" girls who hang on to dancing as long as possible. You may also see them in a hostess bar when the strip club owner tells them to go home or in some fast food restaurant wearing a paper hat.

- *The Over-the-Hill Girls*

These are the dancers I pity the most, the ones who don't understand their career as a stripper is over or haven't made plans to do something else, or don't have the skills to do anything else. As I said strongly above, they never had a Plan B, or their Plan B failed and they didn't have a Plan C. Worst case scenario, they understand they're too old but they're so addicted to the stripping lifestyle, they can't get out. For whatever reason, please God, don't ever let this be me! Usually, they walk around trying to cadge drinks from customers who ignore them or rudely tell them to get lost. They might even try to get on stage to everyone's dismay and go through the motions of dancing…...for no customers. I honestly don't know how they can go home after working all night with little or no money to show for their efforts and not get depressed. What's even harder to understand is how they can come back into work the next night or why the management lets them come back. We have one such girl in our club now. She's in her late 40s and I know she has children and a family because she talks about them. She walks around in the club in outrageous outfits that often include a large white cowboy hat, all in an attempt to get noticed.

But, no matter what she wears or how much make-up she layers on, the wear and tear on her body and face from years of dancing are readily apparent. She just looks old! On the surface, she displays a bubbly personality, sometimes bordering on brash (or desperate), which I think more than anything else gets her a few Lady's drinks each night from customers who pity her. I think the owner also pays her to be the mother hen of the other girls, or in Asian terms - the *mama-san*. And she does do that. She helped me one night when I got totally blitzed sitting with one of my steady customers all night. I actually passed out while I was sitting with him. After letting me sleep for a while, he called this older girl over and she helped me to the dressing room where I promptly threw up. She also got my phone from my purse and called someone pick me up and take me home which was good because I could barely walk. For just that one act of kindness I can pretty much forgive her other vices and peculiarities such as trying to cadge drinks from my customers while I'm sitting with them. One of my steady customers said this girl tried to get him to go up to the Champagne Room with her promising all sorts of sexual favors. Hmmm. He told me there was not enough alcohol in this world to get him to do that. Trying to steal drinks and customers is a blatant violation of an informal professional courtesy we girls observe among ourselves which I'll talk more about next. I guess a girl has to do what a girl has to do which is why I don't get too upset with her, especially if my customers take it in good humor. I have to say again, Please God don't let me be one of these over-the-hill girls...I'm already 31....DAMN.

Dancing Customs and Rules

I'll be the first to admit it's every girl for herself in the Hot Zone; in essence we're all independent contractors. Sometimes that's the beauty of it; it's totally up to us how much money we'd like to make. If we want to dance for a few songs and then take a smoke break, OK, but it's money out of our pocket when we're not on stage. It gets a little more contentious when the club has a lot of customers, like on a Saturday night, and all the dancers want to be on stage to make money. This makes it hard to take a pee break on a busy night especially if there isn't enough stage area for every dancer that's in the club. As bad as that sounds however, particularly when you think of the potential for cat fights between dancers fighting for territory, it isn't total chaos. There are rules, unofficial to be sure, that instill some order into the process and make our lives just a little easier, and most importantly, keep the dancers from attacking each other (although the customers may enjoy that). It should be emphasized these are not just Hot Zone rules but general rules you'll find throughout Hawaii and the Pacific. For all I know they're universal. It's only good business if dancers or hostesses are not at each other's throats all of the time. Better for the girls and better for the customers. Here are some of the rules we live by:

- *Thou Shalt Not Steal Another Girl's Customer*

This is probably **THE** golden rule. Anyone who has ever traveled throughout the Far East will attest this is an international rule observed in every country where girls rely on customers for their income. If you are sitting down with a customer who is buying you Lady's drinks, you should be able to safely leave for a bathroom or smoke break and still find your customer sitting alone when you return. That's not to say he may leave if you take too long, but by God if he does wait, another dancer will not (or should not) be there with him. Now if he had asked her to sit with him, bad on you for taking too long. But if this other dancer has any sense at all, she'll wait and ask you if it's OK; it's what I' do in that situation. Why? First it will prevent the other girl from leaping on you when she comes back and trying to kick your ass. Second, because what goes around comes around. If you screw someone out of a customer, the dancer you screwed is going to look for an opportunity to return the favor and so will all her friends. And <u>you will have to</u> take a bathroom break at sometime during the night. Ha Ha. By the way, this rule also extends to the stage. If you're sitting on the stage with no customer and the girl next to you is dancing for someone who seems to have a lot of dollar bills in hand and a willingness to spend them, you <u>do not</u> slide over uninvited and start dancing for him too. The money he has <u>is for</u> the girl that started dancing for him first, <u>not you</u>….that is of course, unless he looks your way and begins to voluntarily slide dollars into your garter too. Even then, you need to make a show of reluctance to his original "dancing partner" and get a go ahead nod from her. Usually, if she's already got a garter full of dollar, she won't mind a little co-dancing, especially if he continues to stuff dollars into her garter. If she hasn't made much money yet, then you try to politely decline the customer's offer. The bottom line is the girl that's dancing for him may not have a lot of say about who he spends his money on, but you can do her a favor and ensure her customer stays focused on her. The customer may get up and leave at that point, but you've made a friend for life, someone who will help watch your back and return the favor someday.

- *Thou Shalt Not Ask a Customer to Buy You a Drink When He's Sitting with Another Dancer*

This is related to rule one, but not the same. I've had other dancers slide into my booth and blatantly ask the guy I was sitting with to buy them a drink...all of this right in my face. If it's a young dancer doing it, in essence, she's saying to me, "I'm hotter than you." Over-the-Hill dancers won't hesitate to do this as an act of desperation. I had a Vietnamese friend, an aging dancer who is now my former friend, try to do this to me earlier this year. You notice I used the word FORMER. I had been sitting with a customer for about 20 minutes when she decided to pay us a visit. With good humor (on his part, not mine), he was soon buying both of us drinks and rapidly running out of money. Worried about that, he told us that he would only continue to buy me drinks. Remember me, the original girl he was sitting with? Apparently, my soon to be ex-friend forgot that. She got angry and began calling me names and I started screaming back at her. It wasn't pretty and I'm now ashamed at my reaction to her. Similar to the yelling match I described earlier with our bartender, I don't think I left any "F" word form unused, I tend to do that when I'm really upset. My customer left, embarrassed, sometime in the middle of the screaming match which made me even angrier. I vowed to myself I would never again allow one of my fellow dancers to make me lose my cool…it just wasn't my style, well, mostly not my style. My BITCH ex-friend is still my ex-friend although I think she's realized the error or her ways. In both of these "Thou Shalt Not" Commandments, it should be noted that the "Over-the-Hill" girls are generally the most blatant offenders in their desperation to make money, any money. And they mostly get away with it because the dancers pity them. Most times, customers take these Commandment violations in stride and to their credit they may actually concede and buy a couple of drinks before shooing the intruder away so they can concentrate on the business at hand, us younger, sexier dancers. GRIN.

- *Thou Shalt Not Move a Fellow Dancer's Dance Pad*

All of the dancers use small cushioned pads to protect their knees from the hard surface of the stage. If we didn't, we'd have bruises all over our knees. Each dancer has a uniquely personal and recognizable pad. Some make their own pad; others buy them from a lady who comes into the club selling them. As I said before, a dancer will occasionally leave the stage during the night to use the bathroom or take a smoke break. The smoking is a choice, the bathroom break is one of nature's little necessities. Although she's not on a stage, she'll leave her dance pad as a place holder until she returns. Normally, that's not a problem, particularly if the girl is quick. But there are times when the club is crowded and the dancers all want to be on stage at the same time to make money. During these crowded periods, it can be very tempting for a dancer to move an empty dance pad to make room for her pad. Some will only move the pad a few inches which is OK; others will actually shove the pad off the stage which isn't OK. Tensions can really rise when a dancer comes back only to find her pad on the floor and no room for her to move it back onto the stage. Thankfully, this is not a common occurrence. Usually, the dancers are careful about adhering to this "Thou Shalt Not" rule and will conscientiously work around the empty pad knowing that the pad's owner will soon return. And why shouldn't they, everyone has to pee at sometime or other. Again, the driving enforcement mechanism for this Thou Shalt, like other similar unofficial rules, is "what goes around, comes around."

- Thou Shalt Not Talk Stink about a Fellow Dancer

I put this in Hawaiian terms, which means don't say something bad about a fellow dancer. Don't talk about her costumes, don't gossip about her love life, and sure as hell don't talk about her looks. Period. This is one of those "do unto others" biblical warnings. In other words, don't say something bad about a fellow dancer if you don't want them returning the favor. Don't even insult another dancer even though you know she can't hear you because there are no secrets in the Hot Zone. She will hear about what you said eventually if not from a waiter then from another dancer who was nearby when you stupidly said it. Or your idiot customer may tell her just to see her reaction. And then the fight is on. Pretty soon other insults will be uttered, fellow dancers forced to take sides, and sometimes punches actually being thrown and hair pulled. It is just not worth it. It's especially not a good thing to begin throwing stones at someone if you have secrets to hide, because sure as hell the other girl will find out about your secrets and your reputation will be shot when she begins blabbing them. And we all have our secrets…right? So, my rule is: If a customer or another girl asked you about so and so, I respond like any movie star: "She's my best friend and a wonderful person", or "she is a wonderful dancer", all with a big, sincere smile on my face. I'm giving you this advice, because from bitter experience, I don't like working in an environment where another dancer is out to get me.

- *Thou Shalt Not Drop a Dime on a Fellow Dancer*

This is kind an addendum to the "Don't Talk Stink" rule above. We all have secrets we don't want anyone to know about. Exotic dancers probably have more than most because of the life we live. For example, we don't want our real names blabbed to any customer without our prior approval. Reason? We don't want them looking us up in the phone book or the Internet White Pages and then dropping by our apartment. Most of us have a significant other, either a boyfriend or husband. We don't want that known to our customers because they keep coming to see us in the hope of dating and seducing us. They would stop showing up if they knew we were already involved with someone else. One big secret we really don't want divulged is the fact most of us do private shows outside the club. I'll talk more about that later, but needless to say our asses would be fired if management found out. Management probably already knows because they're not stupid. Private shows are common events and the girls have to come from somewhere. They just don't want to officially know. The bottom line to this is: one dancer should not divulge private information on another dancer for any reason. Period. Even though the temptation might be great if there is a spat between the two dancers, but by this rule, neither will (or should not) give any private information on the other to another dancer, customer, or management…again, period. Why not? Because it makes for a bad working environment and a lack of trust. Our jobs are bad enough as it is, we don't need to make it more difficult. And if you do squeal on someone else, as the saying goes, paybacks can be a bitch. For one thing, the offended girl probably also knows stink on you and will proceed to let it fly to your embarrassment. Also, another possible path of revenge could come in the form of the offended girl seeing you in civilian live (outside the club) and publically asking you about dancing nude. This could be very bad if you're with your parents or a new boyfriend. So, to repeat - ***thou shalt not drop a dime on a fellow dancer*** …. keep the gossip to yourself.

- Legalities

Most customers think visiting a strip bar is easy with nothing more complex than buying a drink and watching women get naked? Brother, are you wrong! There are a lot of rules and regulations mandating the conduct of both customers and dancers. A word of warning, a violation of some of the regulations **can result in either the customer or the dancer, or both getting arrested**. It is a well choreographed Kabuki dance...so PAY ATTENTION! If you remember, I was arrested a few years ago so read and heed, I'm an expert on this. There will be a test later...Ha Ha. To start, let's be honest, what most of the girls do in the Hot Zone isn't really dancing. Sure there is music and we move around somewhat in synch with it (some of us better than others), but the music just sets the tone for us to expose our bodies to a customer through various poses. Our goal is to get the customer horny and willing to spend his hard earned money on us, if not on the stage than in a booth or one of the private rooms. As I said before, we want his little head thinking of having sex with us and controlling his wallet. But that's as far as it goes, so says the law...period. There are regulations the dancers and their customers HAVE to abide by, or get arrested. Clubs have been fined heavily and closed down because of repeated violations of these simple rules. First and foremost:

- No Touching

This is THE biggie. Simply put, customers and dancers can't touch each other, ever. This applies anywhere in the club, whether the dancer is on stage or just walking around the club. But illegal or not, dancers are constantly fending off perverted customers trying to touch them. A couple of favorite tricks these perverts use when we dance for them (once…there are no return engagements) are rubbing the back of their hand on our punani as they put a dollar into our garter or folding the dollar and rubbing it on our boobs and punani before putting it into the garter. Although we have bouncers to not so gently escort these perverts out the door, a dancer may give the customer a warning for a first offense before calling the bouncers. If the customer tries to touch the dancer again, then the bouncers gets some work. It's a judgment call for the dancer. We may opt to give a customer a second chance because if we had every customer that touched us or tried to touch us kicked out, there wouldn't be any customers left; it's just the price of doing business in our profession…to a point. On the other hand, there are offenses and there are offenses. One of my fellow dancers had a pervert stick two of his fingers into her punani while she was dancing. She slapped him hard and yelled at him but didn't call a bouncer. Why? Because she wasn't "pulchritudenly" blessed and struggled getting paying customers so she was a little more lenient with perverted customers. Of course the idiot tried it again because he got away with it the first time…and then got kicked out. I think she was very wrong in this incident. I can and do put up with incidental touching here and there and I pretty good at making sure it never happens again. But someone sticking their fingers in me goes way beyond the pale into illegal sexual assault territory. Not only would have I have called the bouncer while I was slapping the shit out of the moron, I would have also called the police…of course, waiting a couple of minutes while the bouncer kicked his ass.

The regulations that apply to customers touching the dancers also apply to dancers touching the customers. Yes it happens, and I'm guilty of it. Shocked? I don't mean the extreme types of touching such as giving a lap dance or fondling his dick. THIS IS STRICTLY A NO NO in Hawaii. The Hot Zone is very conscious of this prohibition and watches its dancers very closely to make sure they don't cross this line. If a customer wants to be touched inappropriately, then he needs to go to some of the more down and dirty strip clubs (like my first club) and hostess bars. Where I sometimes get in trouble with the club is with more innocent touching such as holding his hand or lightly caressing his arms, neck, etc while dancing. I think this physical contact is harmless and a beneficial tool to getting a customer into an intimate relationship frame of mind and more willing to spend money to continue our relationship for that evening. Most of the dancers do the same thing. It's illegal, and we know it, but the club generally overlooks it or at worst, the club manager will walk over and gently remind us to stop, especially if they anticipate a Liquor Commission inspector coming into the club. The rules for touching are a little more lax for dancers sitting with customers in booths because of their close proximity to each other in the small confines of the booth. Common sense dictates the limits of the touching here. Hand holding is OK if there isn't a liquor commission or vice squad inspector about. If that happens, the dancer and customer are asked to move apart as much as possible until the inspector leaves. Lap dances and hand jobs should not even be considered and the dancer is being stupid if she thinks she can make some quick money doing it. And no, a napkin in a customer's lap doesn't adequately conceal hand action. That's been tried before and failed. It's also very hard to conceal the stupid grin on the customer's face and the ahhhhhh everyone in the club can hear when he cums...Ha Ha.

Dancer-customer interactions are checked and enforced in a number of ways in the Hot Zone. Clubs managers walk around the club frequently watching for activity that will get the club in trouble, like a girl giving a customer a hand job. They're also on the lookout for any dancer getting drunk which could set the stage for her doing something stupid. The Table Dance and Champagne Rooms are strictly monitored because there is more money being spent in both places than on the dance stages. The club's owner also walks through the club frequently. He's gently reminded me about not touching customers on a number of occasions. They're gentle because as I said earlier, it's just stroking an arm or neck in the course of my dancing, not jerking someone off...so get your mind out of the gutter...again. Dancers caught doing something blatantly illegal, like a hand job, are fired on the spot with no questions asked. Then there are the Liquor Commission inspections and the vice cops. I talked about them earlier in the book. It's routine for a hostess club to get raided and all the girls being arrested. This doesn't happen in the Hot Zone because the laws are strictly enforced here. If there is a Liquor Commission guy on the premises, the club employees and dancers are well drilled in strictly adhering to the "no touch" rule. In case you're wondering, these Liquor Commission visits are not done secretly. An inspector will arrive at the club front door and announce who he is. When he does, a signal will go into the club for everyone to immediately clean up their act. Only the very stupid are at risk with this type of an open inspection. I think this courtesy is partly a result of the excellent reputation the Hot Zone has for being a class act and recognition of the club management for vigorously enforcing the rules. Vice cops are a little harder to spot. Ask me, I know. Ha Ha. So the bottom line for everyone concerned, club management, employees, dancers, and customers is not to do anything illegal. People can fined or arrested, incomes lost, and lives disrupted. I learned my lesson as I told you, and will never do anything illegal again. Working in the Hot Zone certainly helps in that respect because the management actively discourages any illegal activity, unlike my first club where this type of activity was almost expected and certainly not discouraged by the club management. Anyway...enough said. You can tell this is a sensitive subject with me.

- *No Lewd Dancing*

No lewd dancing??? Isn't that what I do for a living? Here I am naked every night with my legs spread showing customers my most secret places from every conceivable angle, places only my mother and gynecologist should know about.... and I have to worry about not being lewd?? So what is lewd? Basically defined, it's a dancer touching herself. <u>Yet another no touching rule!</u> A dancer can't fondle her boobs or spread herself with her fingers. No fingers inside of anything, probably not even inside your nose. Ha Ha. No masturbating. Get the picture? Horny now? Ha Ha. You can show a customer whatever you like with his face less than a micron from your punani....you just can't SHOW him your internal organs if you have to spread yourself with your fingers to do it. Speaking of showing all of yourself to customers, one of my fellow dancers was very embarrassed one night when she danced for a medical doctor, a proctologist to be exact. As she was spreading her legs for his benefit, he yelled to a fellow doctor who had come into the club with him to come over and take a clinical look at her hemorrhoids, remarking for all to hear how big they were. That happened two years ago and she still mutters about it. It should be a rule that no doctors are allowed in any strip clubs. Not sure I've ever seen a gynecologist in the club; I guess they see too much punani at work and coming into the club would just seem like another day on the job. Maybe they could write off a night out at the Hot Zone on their taxes as a professional training seminar. Ha Ha. Maybe us girls could request a free physical exam from them while we dance. Ha Ha. I'm just waiting for one of these dudes to come into the club with a speculum. You can see that I take this rule less than seriously. Our job is to arouse a customer and if a little lewdness is required, then we do it quietly and quickly. I am not above a quick finger spread if I see it will result in more money in my garter. Couple that with a pouty, come hither smile...Cha...Ching!

- No Kissing Customers

This is the last rule I'll talk about. To put it bluntly, it's stupid. I don't think a lot of brain power was used to come up with this rule so, like the lewd dancing rule above, I don't take it all that seriously; but I still need to mention it. Dancers are not supposed to kiss their customers. Say what?? We're in a sociable business so how can you not kiss a customer goodbye after he just spent a lot of money on you? You want to show him you had a good time (even if you didn't) and you want to encourage him to come back and spend more money on you. Grabbing his crotch would certainly do the job but that's not allowed. Shaking hands is certainly legal, but it's really impersonal and doesn't seem to do an adequate job of saying you enjoyed getting naked for him. You wouldn't just shake hands with a boyfriend would you? So it has to be a kiss. The solution the club accepts? He can give you a chaste kiss on the cheek or you can kiss him just as chastely, or you can kiss each other...chastely of course, you know...like you would kiss a family member...on the cheek. That is assuming you're not weird and don't put the tongue to a family member. If you do....EUWWWW....as the cliché red neck joke goes...do you attend family reunions to get a date? Of course, I've never broken the "no kiss" rule...not me. Of course I have...duh... when the situations warrants it. A quick buzz on the lips is not going to bring the world crashing down around our knees... I am such a scoff-law.

- Dating Customers

Dancers are always being asked to go out on dates. It can't be helped because it's an unintended consequence of our focus on pleasing customers. I can see how a customer might like to see us outside the club or think we'd be interested in seeing them. BUT, as a general rule I don't date customers and I think most if not all my fellow dancers follow this same rule. It just leads to grief because if I date someone I've danced for in the Hot Zone, he'll think (wrongly) that because I'm a stripper, any date we have will end up in bed having sex with perhaps a little kink on the side. After all, aren't my morals already compromised...like those of a porn star? They couldn't be more wrong. They don't seem to understand I am a normal girl in a shitty job and they take it very badly when I tell them I don't want to go out on a date let alone have sex with them. The club also strongly discourages dating customers because it can too easily be misconstrued as prostitution, i.e. a girl meeting a customer outside the club for sex. I won't deny that happens; I just don't endorse it. It can lead to too many bad things so it's just not worth the risk. That's not to say I haven't dated a customer occasionally if I really know him well and I really enjoy his company. The temptation is certainly there especially if the customer is good looking and seems to be a good guy despite coming into a club like the Hot Zone. At a minimum, I will give him my phone number and then let him talk me into a date later on or at least open the door for a future date after I get to know him better. In this, I'm a little more honest than some of the other dancers who give out fake phone numbers. However, as I said earlier, my preference is to meet men outside of my stripping life, men who aren't aware of what I do for a living. But as I also said earlier, there's no guarantee these "outside" dates will go any better as they often result in my date getting hurt feelings because I refuse to have sex with him just because he brought me a drink or we had dinner. Is it my imagination or do all men now think sex is a reward for anything they do nice for us...."Hey! I just opened the door for you...let's have sex!!!" Maybe I am getting too old, or maybe that's why I tend to date older men who are a little more gentlemanly.

The Customers.

We've talked about the dancers and the rules they live by, now I'd like to tell you about the different types of customers I've seen over the years. The damn thing is, like the dancers, the survival of a strip club, and on a more personal level – my survival, depends on the continued patronage of our customers and their willingness to spend money. So no matter how creepy or perverted they are, we have treat them with the respect they often don't deserve to keep them coming back. This is certainly no different from anyone who lives by selling a service or a product, but damn it, we're naked when we're doing it, our product is our naked bodies and our service is providing them fodder for their sordid fantasies. I can feel the slime dripping as I write this.

As a general statement to characterize my observations of strip club customers over the years, I can safely say perversion and voyeurism are not limited to any one social or economic class, and women are even starting to climb into the mix. That said, even though I'll sound a little cynical and negative at times when I describe different types of customers, a lot of them are hard working, very polite people and are often pleasant to know and talk to. Most defy the normal description of strip club habitués as being solely mouth breathers like Al Bundy, but not all; the mouth breathers are there and I see them all the time. I do sometimes wonder if some of the customers I've seen are even part of the species of modern man and not throw backs to an earlier model, say hunter-gathers such as Neanderthals who would be very comfortable hitting me over the head with a club and dragging me back to their caves. Trying to categorize the types of customers was a little tricky because division lines can be blurry at times with customers qualifying in several categories depending how they feel a particular night or how much beer they've had to drink. For example someone in my category of Mr. Married Guy can also be classified as a Mr. Shy Guy, Mr. Cool Guy, or even a Pervert. But, I do define the various customer types as a general guide for you to appreciate the breadth of the various types we dance for. Confused…sorry, but it will clear up as you read further. I just suck at defining my approach clearly.

To begin, I need to say right up front that all dancers should be awarded honorary degrees in psychology because we can analyze the type of a customer within seconds of that customer sitting in front of us. We know how they will act and whether or not we're going to get much money out of them. I kid you not, I can do it and I don't think any professional psychologist or psychologist is nearly as skilled as I am in reading body language and facial expressions, or sensing attitudes. But, and here's where I differ from some of my fellow dancers, I am always willing to give someone a chance despite knowing he's going to be a cretin or pervert, something he'll usually prove within seconds after sitting down in front of me. Although I'm nearly always right in my first assessment, customers can fool me sometimes however. One night they can be a total gentleman and the next time I see them a complete pervert or jerk. I don't know if this is a Dr. Jekyll or Mr.

Hyde thing or just the result of something happening to them between the first and second visits. It needs to be said; however, I'm not the same person from night to night either. One night I can be very tolerate of idiots and the next time I dance I'll have no patience for them. I guess like my customers, my mood swings strongly depend on what happened to me that day and how many drinks I've had when I start dancing. If both sides happen to land on happy personas at the same time, I'm happy and he's happy, then we click and pleasure ensues. He keeps grinning when he goes home to jerk off and I grin when I take his money to the bank. It's a beautiful thing...grin...grin. Have any professional psychologists had better results?

There is one more thing I'd like to say before we start. It's something of a pet peeve with me: To the Hot Zone customers: WHAT THE HELL ARE YOU DOING HERE? Especially you married men! GO HOME, spend time with your wives, girlfriends, and/or significant others. Go meet a girl and talk to her. Get involved in a normal relationship. Basically, GET A LIFE! Hanging out in the Hot Zone every night is not sophisticated. It certainly can't be defined as having a life by any stretch of imagination. OK...I feel better now but I've probably ranted myself out of a job....NAH...stripping is a profession that's been in demand as long as there have been humans walking on Earth. I saw a Super Bowl commercial once depicting a caveman accidentally discovering the wheel. The commercial showed the caveman inserting a rod into the middle of the wheel, like an axle, with the implication he was going to use this discovery to improve his life by making it easier to move heavy objects around. However, since it was a beer commercial you just knew it was going to take unanticipated left turn and it did...a sharp one. Instead of attaching the wheel to a wagon, the caveman set the wheel down on its side with the "axle" sticking straight up thus inventing the stripper poll with the final shot in the commercial showing gorgeous cave women pole dancing. What? Didn't I say stripping was an old profession! Go look up Salome. So on that low note...let's get started. I know you are dying to see what category you fall into...I already know...PERVERT!! Ha Ha. To begin:

- Mr. Lonely Guy

I wanted to start with him first because he's one of the most frequent and saddest types of customers. The Lonely Guy is someone who comes into the club primarily to talk to a girl. We get lots of lonely customers every night. They don't want to go home because, well, there's no one waiting for them there, and spending your nights at home ...alone...can be overwhelming at times. I know, I've been there...done that. So, Mr. Lonely comes into the Hot Zone just to rent companionship for a little while. Best of all, he's willing to keep paying if the conversation is good (remember my talking and listening job skills?). Mr. Lonely can also go to one of the hostess bars in town for the same kind of company, except they won't be naked. This is how hostess bars make a living; they have a good supply of ladies willing and able to keep lonely men company for a short while. Why are these men lonely? Maybe their wife left them, or they're having a fight with their wife, or more probably, they've never been able to functionally relate to a regular girl. They may be way too shy to walk up to a girl in a nightclub or on a dance floor and start talking. The fear of rejection is too great. I'm betting a psychologist would say the reason these types of people are more willing to talk to dancers and hostesses than anyone else such as a friend or family relation is because we're non-judgmental and non-threatening…and we won't reject them…well, we won't reject them as long as they have the money to pay for our time. Besides if they told a relative or a friend some of the things they tell me, they would be ridiculed or ostracized from whatever social circle they belong to. I'm also a captive audience, unlike girls they would meet in a regular dance club. I'm not saying the conversations are always deep and riddled with psychological angst, they usually aren't. Most times, we talk about light, pleasant things, something to take their minds off whatever is bothering them, a few minutes of distraction. Quite often; however, when they start to feel comfortable with me, the conversation will actually dive into exactly what is bothering them. This is why I feel like a psychologist sometimes. My customers will complain about how their wives don't understand them, or how their kids are completely out of control. They will complain about their jobs – how they're under paid for what they do or what an asshole their boss is. For my part, I sit and nod, agreeing with whatever they are saying and not offering any critical comments, such as "Dude, you are fucked up." I also need to control my facial expressions so I don't relay pretty much the same message by frowning or squinting in disgust. That they can get from their wives or significant others free of charge. They may not actually want me to comment and just want to bare their soul to someone. I don't think a psychologist could do it any better, all we lack is a couch for the customer to lay on while he's telling us his life story. I think a lot of my fellow dancers would tell you the same thing about talking to their customers, and most have no problem doing it as long as the customers keep feeding the garter while they talk or rent our time by purchasing Lady's drinks. But, and don't let this get out, we do actually care about our fellow human beings. Stereotype buster...Huh? If someone is hurting, you naturally want to help them. It's human nature. I think we perform a greater good by giving these poor misbegotten souls an outlet to blow off steam. I'd like to know how many marriages we've saved or how many incidents of workplace violence we've prevented simply by giving Mr. Lonely a chance to vent. So Mr. Liquor Commission guy think about that the next time you get worked up by the fact I touched a customer on the arm while I was dancing or stroked a shoulder as I'm reassuring a customer his problems will get better. The right reassurance and a feminine touch can go a long way to defuse a lot of stored up tension that may manifest in a more violent way later.

- Mr. Butt Ugly

I was really struggling trying to decide where to talk about the really ugly customers we dance for. More basically, I was even struggling with whether or not to include this section at all because it just seemed rude. However being rude has never stopped me before and I do get a lot of customers who, charitably speaking, have not been physically gifted by God ....so they turn to me for a little personal and social reassurance. And that's not a problem. Truth be told, I feel sorry for them because they know they're ugly, how can they not? They've been told all they're ugly all their lives and probably ridiculed about it as well, especially when they were young. They've been shunned by women who turn down their requests for dates. All of this boils down to loneliness again and a quest for companionship. That's why I'm describing these customers right after Mr. Lonely, because they're just a variant of this general customer type. I didn't include them with Mr. Lonely because ugliness can result in a social exclusion they really have no control over. They can be the most gregarious people in the world but still kept outside of intimate social circles and not getting the companionship any human needs or deserves just simply because of their looks, so they swallow their pride and pay for it... and that's where I come in. Actually, they can be very good customers given the right loving attention. If they have money, they will keep my garter belt full all night just to keep that attention. They're also the easiest customers to talk into buying a Lady's drink so they can bask in the glow of having an attractive girl (me) snuggling next to them. These are the best case scenarios.

On the other side of the coin, there are customers who overcompensate for their ugliness by being too aggressive or boisterous, especially when they get drunk. A psychologist would call this a "coping mechanism." These are the hardest customers to handle because they're already on the defensive and anything you say to control their actions is taken as an insult which leads to further aggressiveness and maybe a personal discussion with our bouncer. Happily, I've only had to deal with a few ugly assholes. Sometimes, given my failure at relationships with "hunks", I wonder if I would be better off marrying an ugly guy. He would certainly treat me like a queen, just being happy for my attention. I also wouldn't have to worry about him cheating on me…who would he cheat with? My question though - would I still be hungry for an occasional "hunk" snack? Maybe when I was younger, but I'm older and more mature now and I think it would be great to have someone who loves me for who I am, an unqualified love. I would even settle for a half way good looking Nerd. Ha Ha. I can teach him things his Mama forgot to tell him about. Ha Ha.

- Mr. Hunk

Ok, if I talk about ugly customers, for a fair and balanced report, I also need to discuss the good looking customers we see. Like the butt ugly guys, the really handsome guys are also the result of genetic whim, but they are grand prize winners in the DNA lottery, being born with handsome faces and great bodies. And the problem is….they've been praised and idolized for these looks all their lives. My first thought whenever I see a Hunk come in is: why is he even in a strip club? Given his looks, he should be able to pick up any girl he want in the numerous legitimate night clubs in Honolulu. So what's wrong with him? If he comes into the Hot Zone as part of a group, say for a bachelor party, then that's totally understandable, but if he come in by himself, hmmmm…it leads me to think there's something amiss under the hood of that beautiful exterior, some personality disorder not visible to the naked eye. And I should know because these are the types of guys I usually find myself on dates with, beautiful but sick. Ha Ha. To tell the truth, it's not hard for me to dance for handsome guys; easier to fanaticize about having sex with them. And if I'm fantasizing, my dancing can be really sexy. So how are they as customers? The reviews are mixed. Some are legitimately nice guys and are a pleasure to dance for, or even be tempted to date. Others? Very conceited and hard to coax money out of. As I said they've been praised for their looks all their lives, so they think they're doing you a favor by letting you dance for them…with very little money coming as a result of that conceit. Aside from discussing exterior looks of these customers, their inner-selves, their id, can also come in a variety of personalities, the hardest of which to deal with is Mr. Pervert, whom I'll talk about later. If it is a Mr. Pervert, then I can certainly see why this guy is here despite his good looks....a normal girl will see through the beautiful exterior after the first date and not want anything more to do with his rotten core. So as a piece of advice for my fellow dancers, if you see a handsome guy sitting in front of you, approach with caution but you will probably make money if you stroke his ego which you know he'll have in abundance.

- Mr. Married Guy

This is a hard category to talk about because there are so many permutations to this genre of customers. They could be in the club on a lark, just to remember what it was like to be single and have access to all the young bodies they see (especially the old married farts); they could be here as part of party – a bachelor party or a group of guys cutting loose after work; or they may be trying to get the old erotic feeling back they've lost after years of having sex with the wife (some even hoping they can carry this feeling back home and actually have sex with the wife). Married customers come in many shapes, sizes, and attitudes. You will see married guys in every category of customer I talk about in this section of my story. Some are ashamed to be in the club and will either take off their wedding ring (leaving the pale "ghost" of the ring where their finger has tanned but the skin under the ring is white) or will try to hide their ring by covering it up with the other hand. Neither works. Others will make no attempt to hide their rings, and indeed, will even talk about their wives and children with you; some even show you their pictures. I have no clue why these types are here. Maybe they're trying to convince themselves they have a happy marriage. Only a few will give you their real names probably fearing the dancers will do a background check on them afterwards to let their wives know their husbands were being bad boys. But that's OK, I don't give them my real name either. I guess we're in a business of anonymity. Ha Ha.

If you remember my rant earlier, I don't really see why any married guy need to be here at all. I know that sounds wrong because they're spending money on me which I never object to, but I still want to tell them to go home, especially if they try to pick me up. Guys, if you are having problems with your wife, sit down and talk to her like you talk to me, work things out. Things won't improve by leaving your wife alone while you're in the Hot Zone watching me dance. The situation really won't improve if she finds out you've been in a strip club – and she will, count on it. And how is the relationship between you and your wife going to improve if you actually manage to pick up a stripper for extra entertainment? If you want to get that old erotic feeling back or put some zing back into your marriage, go rent a porno movie, and watch it – WITH YOUR WIFE. Or invest in Viagra or Levitra, I hear they work great. If you are just here as part of a larger group and to be sociable with your single friends, well OK, but you better hope your wife doesn't find out, HA – again, she will, so enjoy your few moments in the sun now, it will not be shining on you in the dog house.

What I really, really don't understand is the married guy who comes here with his wife. Dude! What are you thinking? If you think it will put some zing into your sex life, then you are living in a fantasy world. Believe me, your wife does not appreciate you taking her here so she can watch you ogle naked girls. She may be smiling on the outside and saying "Honey, that girl is really sexy", but inside she's seething. I can guarantee if you feel the need to bring your wife into the club to revive your sex life you are already a dead man walking. Your marriage is done, you wife just hasn't told you yet - or she's given you blatant hints and you are too thickheaded to understand. At best, she'll leave your ass as soon as you get home. At worst, she'll discover the reason your sex lives suck is she's really into women instead of men and she'll leave you for one – AND THEN TELL ALL YOUR FRIENDS THAT YOU JUST DIDN'T DO IT FOR HER.

Some dancers consider the Married Guy one of the safest of all the customers they see. They may even choose to have one be their Sugar Daddy, a type of customer we'll discuss later. Why, because (1) who is the Married Guy going to complain to when the girls decide to dump him...their wives? (2) Married Guys have reputations to uphold and families to support so they aren't going to act crazy with a girl and get thrown into jail. I will admit some of my best customers are Married Guys. I even have a Married Guy Sugar Daddy who really treats me nice. Did I tell you that despite having wives, Married Guys are desperate for sex with us younger girls...hah, go figure...but who can blame them? Ha Ha. I had one customer who owned a jewelry store promise me a diamond every time we had sex. Now this was an offer I had to think about...but as I said, I don't do sex for money. They may also ask you to go on trips with them instead of their wives as a traveling companion and bed warmer. I can do both...but again, I tell them right up front in no uncertain term….NO SEX. I went to Denver with my Sugar Daddy a few months ago and San Antonio after that. We had a great time even though we didn't get down and dirty. I think he truly likes my company, can't imagine why, I guess I'm a brilliant conversationalist. Ha Ha. Not only did I have a good time without having to spend money on a room and food, he also compensated me for not going into work on a Friday and Saturday. How could I lose? I keep bugging him about accompanying him on his next trip. So am I a traitor to womanhood for consorting with Married Guys, maybe. I'll talk to you a little more about later about my Sugar Daddy and there are mitigating circumstances that makes my relationship with him a little more palatable, but it's probably still wrong. Ladies, what do you think about Married Guys coming into the Hot Zone and watching us dance or trying to establish a relationship with us?

- Mr. Shy Guy

I see men come into the club all the time who are clearly uncomfortable in being here. I call them Mr. Shy Guy. It usually takes Mr. Shy Guy a long time of ogling dancers from the sideline before he works up enough nerve, or enough sperm overload, to actually sit in front of one. I can actually see him working up his courage, usually with the assistance of a quick succession of alcoholic drinks. There will also probably be a couple of false starts or test runs greased by the liquid courage before he actually does the deed. It's painful to watch. Just for fun, I'll try to catch his eye to give him a jolt of courage to come over. Sometimes that works, other times, he'll quickly turn away or avert his face; the same thing will happen if I try to a talk to him. From long experience, I've learned that nature has to take its course before he can make the bold leap of actually sitting down in front of me. As I said earlier, that leap is probably enabled by a sperm overload or a lot of alcohol.

If a shy customer does come over to me, he still won't make eye contact; instead, he'll just stare at my belly button which is about eye level with him and will quickly put money in my garter as soon as I pull it out, usually fumbling the effort of inserting the dollar into the garter because of shaking hands. Sometimes, he'll even be way ahead of my garter rhythm, actually having the dollar bill out and waiting for me, like he can't spend his money fast enough. More probably, he can't wait to leave what is probably an embarrassing situation for him but has decided he can't leave until all his money is spent. He does get more focused when I take my panties off, or at least moves the area of his focus from my belly button to my punani which has now become the center of his life. It's probably the first one he's ever seen up close and personal. I think at this the point he falls in love with me which can get painful when he runs out of money and I stop dancing. Several trips to the ATM machine thereafter are not unheard of. Although I want to laugh at such shyness, in some ways it's kind of refreshing compared to the other assholes standing around the stage. If you treat Mr. Shy Guy nicely, you're guaranteed to see him on many other nights, and with money. The only bad part is he will probably eventually ask me out on a date since he's not experienced enough to see that my kindness and willingness to talk to him is business and not personal. Since, as I said, I have a policy of not dating customers, this can be a very delicate situation that handled badly can result in me losing a very good customer. I don't want to date them but I also don't want to discourage them either. But, most times, no matter what delaying tactics I use, Mr. Shy Guy will eventually get frustrated after two or three visits and stop seeing me anyway. Sad, some are really nice; they just need a little encouragement to be able to deal with more normal girls in a socially acceptable setting.

- The Perverts

Between the time a dancer first steps out on a stage and when she finally hangs up her g-string, she's guaranteed to run into a lot of these types of customers, the Perverts. They're not in the majority, thank God, a lot of the customers I see in the Hot Zone are generally there just to have a good time and for the most part are respectful of the dancers and the club rules. One Pervert; however, can really ruin what was otherwise a good night and I loathe every one I have the misfortune of dancing for. You can tell I have strong feelings about these morons because this is a long section and it takes a lot of words to describe them; basically, they're walking arguments for the benefits of abortions. I firmly believe Perverts come to the club because no self respecting girl would be caught dead with them even if they are very good looking. There are always more than a few in every group of customers standing around the stages and they're not hard to spot. I can't really give you a physical description because they come in all shapes and sizes, but it's an attitude we dancers are finely tuned to pick up. I'm not sure if it's the way they walk or dress - but there's definitely something tangible we can see or sense. It's probably the smirk more than anything else. I keep thinking how much enjoyment I'd get erasing those smirks with the pointy heel of my shoe…or better yet, a 2x4.

So…let's start….hmmmm so many types of perverts…so little space to write about them….

- The Touchers

I mention these morons earlier. Dancers hate Touchers more than anyone else because they constantly push the envelope to see what they can get away with. As I said, they'll accidentally brush the back of their hands against your punani every chance they get as they slowly insert a dollar into your garter. It's for just this reason I keep my garter down by my knees so there is no chance of any "accidental" punani bumping. They will blow on a girl's punani probably believing it turns girls on, a misconception I believe they get by watching tons of porno films because they can't get real girls to have sex with them, or sex with them more than once. The list goes on and on. They won't just insert a dollar into the garter and be done with it. No, they fold the dollar in half and try run it up and down my body first, paying close attention to my boobs and punani before putting it in the garter. I've already told you about the finger in the punani incident with another dancer. In this one specific incident, I'm not sure I have any sympathy for that dancer. An experienced dancer, which this girl was, can see immediately if she has a pervert sitting in front of her and can tell right away they may try something stupid like copping a feel. Then it becomes her job to be alert for the attempt and stop it before it starts. Let me reiterate, it's the dancer's responsibility to be on her toes and be aware that a pervert customer in front of her will probably do something stupid. So if I have one reach out and try to touch my punani, he'll get the immediate sensation of broken fingers followed up with the bouncer's boot up his ass and being held face down on the floor until the police come. Then fun times in jail commence.

I had one moron that kissed any part of my body that came close to him as I was moving around on the stage - my neck, my arms, hands, and butt. I told him once to stop it and when he persisted, he got an assisted trip out of the club. The only problem was I couldn't detach his lips from his face before he got kicked out. I hate to drop a dime on my own sex, but perverts are not confined to just men; women can sometimes be the worst offenders. For some reason they think the NO TOUCHING rule does not apply to them because they're women. WRONG. Some dancers do give their female customers a little more latitude sometimes for physical contact that they wouldn't normally allow a man, but I won't. To me, TOUCHING is TOUCHING and it's a personal insult, a violation of my personal space. Dancing naked leaves little personal dignity to start with and I jealously guard what little I have. That means not allowing any idiot to touch me, man or woman is a rule I strictly enforce.

- *The Weenie Wagglers*

I don't see these types of perverts very often, but every once in a while a customer will get so carried away he'll break out his pathetic little weenies out and begin stroking it while I dance for him in the Table Dance area. I see customers rubbing the front of their pants all the time even on the main dance floor. They can be very slick about it and pretend they're just cleaning something off their hands and scratching their nuts which would be believable if they only did it once, but you they give yourself a vigorous rubbing every few seconds then Dude…you're either spanking the monkey or you have a terrible case of crabs. As bad as that, the Weenie Wagglers are worse, because they've whipped the beast out of its barn for all the world to see. Again….Dude! Didn't your Mommy slap your hand as a child when you reached into your diapers and did that?

I can remember two guys in particular who whipped it out…not together…stupid…just two separate customers that kind of stand out in my memories. They did it while I was dancing for them in the Table Dance area, so I think they were trying to take advantage of the privacy. I was very polite to each of them when I saw what was happening and warned them politely to stop. When they persisted, the club employee watching the Table Dance room made them take the walk of shame out of the club. I have to tell you quite frankly neither guy was lacking in the size department and it was kind of a turn on, but rules are rules. I'm not even sure they were allowed to zip up before having to leave. Ha Ha. If the Perverts that come into the club want to get themselves off, they don't need to choke the chicken (jackoff, spank the monkey, slap the salami, pound the pud….you know what I mean) in public or more importantly in front of me. It's much better for them, and for us, if they buy a porno movie and have at it in the privacy of their own home where they can flog their little weenies to death every night and all day long if needed.

As a variation to the Weenie Waggler, I had one customer who was obviously not from this dimension of reality actually take off all his clothes right in front of me on the main dance floor. The bouncers didn't even give him a chance to get dressed or pick his clothes up from the floor before they escorted him out. He went out of the club in the same condition he came into this world…naked. That I can remember, his clothes stayed on the floor until closing time. To this day, I don't know how he got home naked. Don't care either. It would have been funny though if he was married and had to explain to his wife why he was coming home naked. "Funny you should ask, you see, it was like this….." Ha Ha.

- *The Fetishers*

I'm not even sure "Fetisher" is a word but I use it to mean someone who has a little kink in his sexual make up. I don't really mind this type of perverted customer, kind of amusing mostly. If he wants to lock in on staring at my shoes or my boobs…ok…fine.

It's harmless and if it pushes his buttons then Dude, enjoy! I don't know if it's a fetish, but a lot of customers lock in on my punani. It seems like the rest of my body is invisible to them and my punani is the center of my existence. How can I tell what they're thinking? Easy....I can move my punani up and down, left and right...and their eyeballs follow it like radars locked on a target. Ha Ha. These customers are dead meat when I see this. They might just as well empty out their wallets right then and there for me because all I have to do to get the money flowing is cover my punani and only uncover it after I've gotten a certain number of dollar bills in my garter. It works all the time, just like Pavlov's dogs. Ha Ha.

I had one customer that only had eyes for my feet. I'd heard about foot fetishes but had never seen it in action until this gentleman. He stared at my toes the whole time I danced for him. He paid absolutely no attention to me taking my clothes off, just how my toes wiggled when I moved. I mentioned a customer that was into kissing earlier, this guy had him beat. I had to stop him from trying to suck on my toes while I was dancing a couple of times. I told him you can look…...but not suck...Ha Ha. Damn…I wonder how these fetishes get started. Do I have any fetishes? Nah…as least none that I'll share with you but does whip cream and baby oil bring anything to mind???? Ha Ha….

- Others

I said earlier I can usually identify a pervert almost immediately after he sits down, but I'll be the first to admit that

I've been fooled too. I sometimes think I give my phone number out to customers too easily. If I dance for a guy I like and he asks for my phone number, I'll usually give it to him and will even answer the phone if he calls at least once - unlike most girls who give fictional phone numbers to their customers. Why, do I give out my number? It's good customer relations. If they call and I answer and talk to them, they'll keep returning to the club to see me, especially if I answer their call with a "Hello Sexy." I won't go out with them (at least not usually), but I don't mind talking to them and if I get to know them better after they come to the club several times to watch me dance, I may agree to dinner, but nothing more. Anyway, this habit of being free with my phone number has sometimes caused me problems when I've been fooled and given it to a well concealed pervert. One time, I gave it to a Filipino guy who then started calling me more than a hundred times a day. The few times I answered the phone, all I could hear was heavy breathing. I could tell he was Filipino because I could hear a Filipino TV show in the background whenever he called. He was truly scary and one was of the few customers I really worried about. I tried being nice to him on the phone and then being angry with him, but neither approach had any effect. He just kept calling and calling. I finally stopped answering when I saw his number on my caller ID but that didn't faze him in the least. He kept up his frenetic calling for at least six months. Gradually the calls slacked off to about once or twice a day for another six months and then ended. I quickly forgot about him, but a couple of months later he called me out of the blue and not thinking I answered the phone. Again the silence and I began cursing myself for being stupid. Needless to say, the calls began pouring in again, about several hundred a day. I finally stopped it by dropping my cell phone contract and getting another phone. I feel very sorry for the poor soul the telephone company reassigned my phone number to. I hope it was some big guy named Gunther and he was able to hunt the pervert down and beat the crap out of him. While I'm on the subject of phone perverts and regretting giving out my phone number so easily, for more than a week last year, one of my former customers began sending me pictures of his weenie for some reason. He asked me to visit him in San Diego and when I refused the weenie pictures began to flow into my phone. Yes, he was a remote **Weenie Waggler**. He didn't have the staying power of the Filipino guy; however, and after a week of me ignoring him, his calls ceased. Damn my life is interesting. It wasn't even a big weenie.

- *Open Note to All Perverts*

Maybe you think us dancers get turned on by watching you jerk off or by having you touch us. Do you actually think it will make us want to have wild sex with you? That is so wrong it's tragic. My message to you all is this. "You sad little men, stop it!" Dancers don't appreciate your attentions or your attempts to "turn us on." If you want to come in and watch us dance, then by all means come in and be welcome; after that you can go home and play with yourselves until your weenie falls off IN THE

PRIVACY OF YOUR BEDROOM. Anything else, don't bother. JUST STAY HOME. Our tolerance level of you trying to take liberties with us is very low and we won't hesitate to have you escorted out, or to place charges against you. We may be nude dancers, and as such, don't seem to place very highly in your your list of people to respect, but we're just like you....well, no not just like you on second thought. We're normal. This is a job for us to be able to support ourselves and our families. More to the point is why do you come into the club to embarrass yourself in the first place? Believe it or not, the person lowest on the social totem pole is not us, it's you because it's very evident you're here because you can't find a girl in the normal way. So please do us a favor and as I said before in capital letters – STAY HOME.

- The Jerk

I could have included this moron in any of the other categories of customers I'm describing but I think he deserves to have a section of his own. As a basic definition, a jerk is a customer who thinks he's better than anyone in the club, the dancers in particular. Through his actions and his words, he conveys a self-asserted feeling of superiority. It's as if he's doing you a favor by letting you dance for him. And here's a question for everyone reading this book: describe how you think a Jerk will act when it comes to putting money into a dancer's garter? Answer, he'll be a cheap bastard who'll pinch his dollars as much possible making the dancer pull her garter out several times before he actually let one of his dollars go. So he's a cheapskate which I'll describe later.

And guess what? As a bonus, you can probably bet he's a pervert too. How can I make that assumption? Because you can see right away the only person he holds in any regard is.......HIMSELF. He cares nothing about the dancer as a person, so why should he have respect for her body and personal space? Whenever I see this type of customer sit down in front of me, I just inwardly sigh and try to make it as painless for myself as possible. He won't get any of the normal loving care I give every other customer. For him, I just want him to leave as quickly as possible even if I don't make much money off of him. There are always more customers waiting for my time with a greater willingness to spend their money on me and a better attitude to boot.

- Mr. Condescending

We've all seen this type of guy at sometime in our lives, actually quite often, and we've all wanted to punch him in the face....hard. He's the guy that knows everything about everything and thinks he's way better than you are. Well, we all know how we're perceived as dumb strippers with sleazy lifestyles, so we're natural targets for this turd. I could have easily included Mr. Condescending under The Jerk but you can tell by some of the emotional language I'm using I think this customer more than deserves his own small section in my book. Maybe it's because I'm not stupid I object vehemently to someone who assumes otherwise before I've even spoken a word simply because of my job. This is the type of a guy who won't give you his real name when you ask or who will blatantly try to talk over your head and then laugh if you don't understand him. I don't know why the first words out of his mouth aren't "look I know you're stupider than me, so why don't we just not talk and you get naked." And then they have this "I'm smarter than you" smirk on their face all the time they're sitting in front of me. I think part of the problem is I'm Asian and they assume all the Asians they see in the strip clubs and Hostess bars are just off the ship and aren't well educated or articulate. For the most part they're correct, but even basic humanity dictates you don't rub it in. Besides, more often than not, they'll run into someone like me who is actually more intelligent and better educated than they are. I keep wanting to say…look asshole, I have a college degree and I speak three languages fluently, what can you do? But that's all right. I don't mind keeping my mouth shut and dancing for these assholes, it just takes a lot more time and money to inspire me to take each article of clothing off. Ha Ha.

- *The Show off*

The Show Off is a breed of customer you see coming into the Hot Zone as part of a larger group. The members of this group are his enables, functioning as the audience for his performance, yelling "ohh" and "ah" at his outrageous behavior thus giving him the necessary encouragement for more idiocy, usually at the expense of the dancer. The Show Off will sit in front of a dancer only after he's gotten the full attention of the group or after he's been egged on by the group with a lot of snickering and smirking. Think of a little kid yelling at his parents saying "Look at me!" I hate dancing for a show off moron because I just know I'm going to have a hard time with him and his posse of fools. Ironically, if he came into the club by himself, he probably wouldn't be as bad and may even be a nice guy, but as part of a group he'll play for the group's reaction every time, the greater the reaction the more outrageous his actions will be. It's even worse if the guy is a pervert - that's a double whammy that makes me wish a hammer or some other deadly weapon was part my costume. There are a number of different ways the Show Off will play for his peers: he'll be totally insulting hoping to get a reaction out of me and his buddies; he'll try to see how much he can get out of me for as little money as possible; or he may resort to physical humiliation such as touching my punani (see Pervert). Some dancers will play along by putting on their own performance either by flirting outrageously with him or putting on an exaggerated show for their benefit of his audience. That's not for me. If I see I have a fool in front of me that's the end of the show. I'll get up and move on to a more profitable customer or one that's just interested in me. I don't give a shit about playing along with either the Show Off or his home boyz. I've even been known to call in a bouncer if the Show Off's activities get too far out of line. Then he can entertain his posse by the sight of his ass getting bounced out of the club. Better, they can watch his assed getting kicked if he mouths off to the bouncer. Like me, the bouncers have very little idiot tolerance.

- Mr. Cool

Mr. Cool is the type of customer who projects the image of having been there and done that. Nothing you do impresses him or penetrates his "cool" demeanor. If smoking were allowed in the club, he'd have a cigarette dangling out of the corner of his mouth (left corner only, the right corner is for the common people), alternating between puffs and taking a drink. No beer, a mixed drink only with a name brand of alcohol. He will put a dollar into your garter only when asked several times and will then look offended at the thought that you are only regarding him as a source of income and not a potential romantic conquest. And he won't quickly insert his dollar into the garter; instead, he'll languidly place it there, all while keeping a passive face as if it were the most natural act in the world. Idiot. You can tell that I have no patience for this type of customer any more than I have for any other type of fool. No one is that special and even if Jesus Christ himself sat in front of me, I would still push him to fill my garter. It's a business and I don't like being here, so I'm going to get as much money as I can out of every encounter; so sue me. I'm probably going to hell anyway for my Jesus comment, and if I do, I'll see all of my customer and my friends there…they're all PERVERTs. Ha Ha. And if their wives find out about their predilection for nudie bars, they'll be in hell waiting for me all the sooner. Ha Ha

- The Big Spender

This is THE type of customer every girl hopes she runs into, if ….and that's a big IF, they aren't also perverts. For simplicity purposes, I'm going to talk about the non-perverted kind, because rich or not, I won't have anything to do with perverts. I'm not talking about the usual customers who will sit down in front of you and spend maybe $20 to watch you dance or maybe buy you a couple of drinks. No, what I'm talking about here is a guy who comes in and drops several hundred dollars. THE BIG SPENDER. He's a guy who's either rich to start with or has just come into a temporary bunch of money and is out to have a good time. Girls, for longevity, the rich guy is a godsend if he takes a liking to you….isn't very demanding…and importantly, isn't a pervert or a FLAKE which quite frankly seems to happen a lot. If he meets these criteria and he's a normal, likeable guy with money, then see my Sugar Daddy discussion below because that's what you'll want him to become. If he becomes a Sugar Daddy he may spend thousands on you over the long haul because he cares about you. You don't have to fall in love with him but you do have to make him feel loved. It helps a lot if you actually like him, but treat him with all of the savvy and girly wiles you've gained over the years and you won't regret it. There is a reason he's sitting in front of you and there's a reason you want him to keep coming back and sitting in front of you, he'll have a fist full of dollar bills and a willingness to deposit them in your garter. With enough gentle persuasion he'll also be good for a lot of Lady's drinks and maybe even the whole night of Lady's drinks. The bottom line is he will keep you off of the dance floor and you'll be making money at the same time. To my mind when I get one of these customers, I've hit a JACKPOT, especially if I can convince him to come in regularly (on nights that my other steady customers don't come in on…Ha Ha) and spend money on me.

I've talked about the rich, steady guy, now let's talk about the customer that fell into some money and wants to have a good time. In many ways, this is even better than the rich guy because with his "I've got a lot of money to burn and I want a good time" attitude you can get him to spend a lot of money on you in a very short time for dancing and Lady's drinks and possibly the Table Dance room or even better, the bigger score of the upstairs Champagne room. The income from this adventure could set you up for the entire month. You may have to beat back some wandering hands but the end profit will be worth the effort. And, chances are, he'll go along with whatever you tell him or want him to do. Unlike the rich guy who has some basic intelligence (or rather a lot of intelligence), this "have a good time guy" is just in the moment and not looking for a long time relationship. So he's as temporary as you are, as long as the money and the booze keeps flowing. The one drawback is he may spend all of his money leaving nothing behind. I had a customer like this last year. He blew everything and got almost too drunk to stay vertical. He couldn't drive home and I wasn't about to let him stay with me or drive him home, so having a conscience, all evidence to the contrary, I paid for a cab out of the money I'd earned from him so he wouldn't be left stranded in our parking lot after we closed. See, I'm not a total Bitch…RIGHT? RIGHT????

My friend the Thai girl had a similar experience with a blow it all away guy. He came into the club last year with a bunch of checks in his hand saying money was no limit. Naturally, the girls flocked to him, too damn bad I had the night off or I would have been first in line...Ha Ha. He was buying Lady's drinks in bunches and was taking not only one but several girls up to the Champagne Room in rotating groups of three or more. Then when he was finished, he handed girls blank checks telling them to fill in whatever amount they felt was appropriate. Well, I know as you're reading this, you're thinking to yourself, there was no way this had a happy ending. Mind readers! You're right...it didn't. It worked OK for the first two or three girls that filled out their own checks and quickly deposited them in the bank, but thereafter, everything else bounced. I did see him a couple of nights after that trying to get girls to dance for him on the cheap. Surprisingly (I'm being sarcastic here), the dancers weren't so accommodating. There is a popular Filipino bar girl saying for this: "*Walang Pera, Walang Mahal*." In English, "No Money, No Honey." I think that little nugget of wisdom should be recorded in some historically significant place for everyone to benefit from, how about as part of the Ten Commandments? Now I know I'm going to hell, but it's an acknowledged universal truth like all the other Commandments. Any single guy will testify to that. Any girl will also. After all, what girl wants to go out with a guy that has no money....and who probably wants sex on top of it. It's a wonder the human race has managed to breed and populate the earth.

- *The Cheapskate*

This is the type of customer dancers really hate. He is the absolute counterpart to the Big Spender. He may be the nicest, most polite person in the world but all that is negated if he's reluctant to part with his money. Rich or poor, it doesn't matter; if he doesn't want spend the money for our time or doesn't have the money in the first place, then he shouldn't be expecting us to dance for him. It's a waste of our time and it actually costs us money. We're in a business after all and we could be dancing for someone who wants to spend money on us instead of this idiot.

As I've said before, I know what type of customer I have right after he sits down. With the cheapskate, I'll be very polite at first and politely tell him I am looking for payment for my efforts when I pull out my dancing garter. If no dollars are forthcoming or they are not forthcoming quickly enough, I quietly stand up and move on to greener pastures, leaving him sitting there with a stupid look on his face. They are lucky in getting my subdued reaction, I've seen other girls take a more direct approach such as pouring the drink the customer had on his head. I want to tell them...."Dude! What alternate world did you come from where you expect a dancer to take off her clothes for free?" In my book, ignorance of how the dancer-customer dynamic works is no excuse. Even the dumbest novice can get a crash course in proper behavior within minutes after walking through the front door of the club just by watching other customers. Chances are good he may have been spoiled in the recent past, probably by a beginner (remember?)

who didn't ask much of him and he expects the same from me; sorry to disappoint. Welcome to the real world. I've got bills to pay and dancing for you for free doesn't get them paid. As I said, my reaction to these cheap fucks is cut my losses in wasted time and walk away, very low key. Predictably, I haven't had one of them call me back by saying "Wait, I was wrong; I'll give you money whenever you ask for it." I probably wouldn't go back anyway, but that's beside the point. While I'm telling you about the cheap guy, let me fill you in on a favorite cheap guy tactic. They will try to sit down in front of me right after I finish dancing for someone else and am still naked. I think they hope to pick up where the other guy left off without having to invest some upfront dollars as incentive for me to take my clothes off in the first place. To prevent this, I'll have my previous customer stay until I finish dressing and then let him leave. If that doesn't work and I see a cheap bastard hurry over to sit in front of me, I'll make him wait until I slowly get dressed and then I'll start my dance routine. It's really funny to see the realization slowly creep onto their faces that they're not going to get to see my punani for free or even cheaply for that matter. I can tell you right now, if I suspect a customer will be a cheap bastard, I'll take my time removing my clothes. It'll cost him more than what I would charge other customers to see my goods. Girls, here's a customer alert to a variation of the cheap guy - the cheap guy who knows what he is and tries to conceal it. He will sit down in front of you with a thick wad of money in hand fronted by a $100 bill. What he won't show you, but what you'll find out soon enough, is there are nothing but one dollar bills behind the $100 and you'll have to toil mightily to pry them out of his hands.

- Customer Tandems

I'm adding this genre of customers rather late in the writing of this book. I'd forgotten about them until I started editing my description of Mr. Cheap Guy above and realized that customer tandems are a variation of the cheapskate approach. I kind of struggled to come up with a name to call them. Tag Teams? Partners? Side-saddlers? Regardless, I see two customers sharing a single dancer all too often. It leaves me wondering what the hell is going on. Why do they feel they need to watch a dancer together? Are they a couple? If that's the case, they're gay, which leaves the bigger question of why they're interested in a naked girl in the first place. Are they so insecure they need the reinforcement of sitting next to each other to work up the courage to have a girl dance for them? I don't think so. I think the better answer is they're cheap bastards trying to enjoy the services of a dancer at half the cost they would normally incur if each watched her alone. If I were a guy, I think I'd like to be alone in my lustful fantasy of ogling a naked girl not sitting next to a friend while I start to breathe hard and get a boner. Getting aroused is not something to be shared with a drinking buddy even if he was also putting money into the dancer's garter. If he has money he can get his own damn dancer. It should be just me and a naked girl sharing an intimate moment...PERIOD. If that ruins our friendship, then so-be-it.

Here's a visual....on life's scale, you have a naked woman asking for your undivided attention on one side and on the other side, your asshole buddy wanting to share that moment with you....hmmm....I'm sorry asshole buddy...you're out. A little further down, I'll describe another two-person combo, but this time couples. I have absolutely no problem with being a shared erotic moment between couples.

- The Nice Guy

At this point, most of the customer descriptions you've read aren't very flattering. Why would you expect otherwise from me, or from any dancer for that matter? What types of people do you think frequent a strip club? Think of Al Bundy going to his local "nudie bar." But as I was re-reading what I had written, I began to think I hadn't completely described all of the customers I've seen. Specifically, I do occasionally dance for genuinely nice guys; some of which I even consider dating...surprised? I've even met some guys where I didn't feel compelled to pull out my garter belt with rapid frequency. I actually wanted them to stay and talk even though there were lots of other customers hovering around trying to rent my time. You say, hard-hearted Amaya giving a customer a break...and ignoring other customers? Well, yes on a few occasions...a few, rare occasions. OK, I'll wait until you pick yourselves up off the floor.......waiting.......waiting......waiting. Now that you're back, I'll tell you that these nice customer are few and far in between, but even still, because of them, I can't totally get away with saying all Hot Zone customers are perverts, cheapies, and other ill-begotten sons of humanity. What make them seem nice in my eyes? I can't list any specifics, I just know immediately when a nice guy sits down. A gut feeling? A smile, or some "nice guy aura." Maybe. It could also be just a lack of general creepiness when you compare him with the other losers standing in a crowd next to the stage. To soothe your feelings of betrayal by me liking some customers or being willing to date one even if it contradicts my oft stated general no date policy, none of these nice guys have ever become a boyfriend or even a steady friend, most not lasting longer than a single date. In their defense, they didn't suddenly turn into creeps, we just decided we had separate interests outside of the Hot Zone and went separate ways. That's not to say they don't return to watch me dance occasionally, they do, and we have a good time. Some have even turned into the type of customer I'll describe next, the Loyal Customer. One, just one only, went on to become a Sugar Daddy which I'll discuss after the Loyal Customer.

- *The Loyal Customer*

Like the Big Spender, this is another type of customer every dancer likes to get. A Loyal Customer is defined as someone who routinely comes into the club just to see a specific girl. He will probably have an established routine of coming in on the same day and time and if his favorite dancer is smart she'll be ready for him when he arrives. I usually take a bathroom break about fifteen minutes before I expect one of my loyal customers. That way I won't be busy with another customer when he does walk through the front door of the club. I've seen dancers go so far as sending texts to their loyal customers coordinating the days the customer can come in and find her dancing. This thoughtfulness ensures the customer won't waste his time coming in when she's not there. More selfishly from the girl's perspective, he won't come in and find another dancer to shift his loyalty to in her absence. Ha Ha. I can't laugh, I do the same. Even more conveniently, I have one customer who texts me when he's coming in and giving me a countdown of when he'll arrive so he can be assured I'll be waiting for him and not dancing for someone else which he hates watching. Dancers also text loyal customers if they're having a slow day wanting to know if they have time to come in now. I'm not sure what drives my loyal customers, maybe my sparkling personality or witty conversational skills, Ha Ha, but I'm not complaining. I have several that routinely come into see me. They may not be able to spend a large amount of money on me in a single night like the Big Spender I described above, but they are a steady source of income you can always count on, and mostly, they're really nice people I enjoy dancing for. I do have one loyal customer that does spend a lot of money on me. I call him Mr. Champagne Room. He lives in Los Angeles and routinely comes to Hawaii on business every few months. Before he comes, he'll either call or text me telling me the day and time he'll come into the Hot Zone. When he gets here, he immediately takes me to the Champagne Room where he'll purchase one or two bottles of champagne. As I said, the Champagne Room has a number of video camera ensuring no sex happens, and it doesn't with this customer, but he's not there for the sex anyway. Don't get me wrong, I do get naked. But he likes to talk to me and we have great conversations. For him, I make an exception to my "No Dating the Customers Rule." He'll take me out to eat and he'll also take me as his escort to his business functions. When we go to a function, he'll compensate me for income lost when I'm not dancing and he'll also give me money to buy clothes appropriate for the function we're going to. Usually, we have a great time but there was a problem the last time he came. He took me to some business function that was also attended by his daughter. She came over to our table and introduced herself to me. She was pleasant enough but I heard her whisper to her Dad, "What about Mom?" That shot me through the heart and my relationship with my Champaign Room customer never recovered. He called a couple of weeks ago and I didn't answer the phone. He hasn't called since.

Back to my other loyal customers. The only problem I experience from time to time is when they come in at the same time; I've had as many as three stacked up waiting for me. Mostly they're nice about it, at least on the surface, but it can get a little tense, and I sometimes feel pressured to hurry the one I'm with so I can move on to the next one. I'm sure the customer I hurried leaves the club just a little disgruntled because he wanted to spend more time with me …but I haven't lost a customer yet. Again, my sparkling personality?…nah, more probably because if I short someone I'm really nice about it and I make a note to spend more time with him the next time he comes in. I'll also try to take it a little easier on him with Lady's drinks, at least for a little while. A recent example of this happened this last weekend. I had a long time steady customer waiting for me when I first walked into the club. He started buying me Lady's drinks whenever I asked for them and even got me some food. I was thinking this was going to be a great night. Then the problem came in the form of another steady customer who decided to also pay me a visit. What to do? What to do? The solution really boiled down to economics. Normally, it would be first come, first served, but this second customer likes to give me $20 for every song I dance for him (in other words he fills my garter with a lot of money at a rapid pace). The economics? With the first guy, I was averaging a Lady's drink about every 10 minutes, of which I shared the income from the drink 50-50 with the bar. So math majors, I was making $10 every ten minutes – or breaking it down further, $1 a minute. With the second customer, I get $20 for every song I dance for him. Given that songs average about 3.5 minutes in length, I make a little under $6 a minute. Result? My profit is much higher with the customer who pays me for dancing than the one buying me Lady's drinks. Guess which one I decided to spend more time with? ECONOMICS. I bet you didn't think nude dancing would have all of these high financial considerations did you? Ha Ha. Rest assured, I was very nice to the first customer as I was walking him out the door. Not wanting him to feel too put out, I kissed him and promised he would have a better time when he came in again. Did

I tell him about the second customer? No…are you stupid? After all, he was a good customer and I wanted him to come back. I lied my ass off and told him the management was short handed with dancers that evening and told me to go back on stage even though I was sitting with a customer. It's happened in the past so my lie was totally believable. And I had every intention of getting back on stage…to dance for my higher paying customer.

As a final note. I do have a promotion system in place for my customers. A Nice Guy customer can get promoted to Loyal Customer with hard work and total devotion to me. One, and only one of my Loyal Customers may have a chance to be promoted to Sugar Daddy but this takes a lot of hard work, devotion to me, a lot of money spent, and….when I have an opening. I have only one Sugar Daddy position at this time. I think any more will be too difficult to manage, they can get kind of demanding at times…Ha Ha. When I do have an opening, the interview process can be a bitch….with me being the bitch….Ha Ha. Having a Sugar Daddy is the ultimate goal for any dancer… which coincidentally, I'm going to discuss next.

- The Sugar Daddy

Sigh…this is a hard one for me to write about because, as I've said, I have one, and damn me if I don't care about him which goes against all of my rules. The definition of a Sugar Daddy may differ a little from dancer to dancer but it's generally an older man who falls in love with you for some reason. They should know better but they don't. They will spend a lot of money on you until they finally have an epiphany about how stupid they're acting or they get tired of you not returning the affection they expected for their attentiveness. Generally, but not always, the Sugar Data urban legend is these older men are generally well off financially and therefore they can afford the money they spend on the girl. Every girl has a number of Loyal Customers if she dances long enough, each always seeking her out when they come into the club and each always willing to spend money on her. The Sugar Daddy transcends the Loyal Customer because he's looking for more of an emotional connection, and sometimes finds it. I can't think of any dancer who wouldn't mind having a Sugar Daddy, in fact a lot of them do. The differences come in how they react to an older man suddenly wanting more than just watching them dance, he wants a piece of their personal life. A lot of dancers just simply accept the affection and the monetary rewards and do return a certain level of affection or at least some physical benefits; if they don't, the man will move on to someone else to fall in love with. I have a Sugar Daddy, his name is James. I've known him for the last five years, remarkable longevity considering how short all my other relationships have been – reference husbands one and two. He's almost twice my age, in fact he is twice my age; he just turned 61 as I write this book. I must have a thing for mature men; my second husband was much older than me. Maybe I like their maturity when compared to the boys I usually go out with. I met James one night while I was dancing on stage. He came over and started talking to me in Tagalog, my native Filipino language. I told him later I thought it was weird seeing my language come out of a white guy's mouth. He was respectful, had a good sense of humor, and certainly wasn't tight with the money. In talking to him, I found out he was a retired Navy officer who had lived for ten years on the Navy base in Subic Bay, Philippines. He was also married to a Filipino wife for more than 30 year. So why was he in the club? His wife was on an extended stay in the Philippines building an apartment building for retirement income. For the five years that I've known him, she's been in the Philippines at least nine months out of each of those years. Sometimes it makes me mad when he tells me the reason he sees me is because he gets lonely when she's gone. Ok, but then I give him hell for letting her go for such a long time in the first place or not going to see her. He has no answer for that other than she's as strong of a woman as I am (he says hard headed) and telling her no would have no effect on her other than making her mad and his life miserable. I just think he happier when she's gone then when she's home with him here in Hawaii. Why do I think that? Because he also sees me when she's home, sneaking out from his work at lunch. So, I'm not sure they have much of a marriage any longer. I know that's rationalizing, but there you have it. But he is a very good man and very devoted to me.

Anyway, we've had this strange relationship for the last five years. With him, I've broken two of my major rules – don't date the customers and more importantly, don't mess around with married men. But I go out with him all the time anyway, he's funny, entertaining and most importantly he's patient with me. I've driven away everyone I care about in the past with my temper and intolerance of stupidity. Sometimes, I'm my own worst enemy in a relationship. I want to love someone but I don't want to let them take over my life. James just lets me rant and cuss him out and then when it's all over, smiles and proceeds to make me laugh to ease the tension. He says I don't even come close to the quality of ass chewings he got in the Navy or gets routinely gets from his wife. James is the customer I told you about earlier that has access to my inner most secrets because we've been together so long. If he sees me being particularly bitchy, he won't hesitate to drive right down to my inner self to make me cry. He says it's like popping a blister with me. He'll get me furious and then stand back and wait for the storm to blow over. As I said, the Hot Zone waiters and bouncers are used to this and also take shelter. After that, I'm fine and James and I proceed to have a good time. One night, after I was particularly irritated with him because we'd had a fight, I sent him a text as he was driving home telling him to "fuck off and die." He just let it slide and the next day sent me a text saying he loves me. Go figure. With him, I've even relented and apologized after yelling at him and sending him other heated text messages. I don't apologize very often, so this puzzles me. He says he feels flattered when I get mad at him and send him texts with inventive drop dead messages. He says it shows I have emotions for him or I wouldn't even bother being mad at him, I would just drop him like I've done everyone else. I think he's right. I've certainly given him more slack that my other relationships. Oh well, it hurts my head to think about it.

James supports me a lot financially. He buys me groceries, clothes, make up, and pays to have my nails and hair done. We've established sort of a comfortable set routine over the years. He comes into the Hot Zone about 7 pm on Friday nights and stays with me until 10:30, buying me Lady's drinks and food. He also pays me a lot of money when I dance for him. He always brings flowers for me and food for the rest of the dancers. The other dancers have a love/hate feeling about him. They love the food he brings it and will all visit our table to eat; they also hate that he brings the food because they're all on perpetual diets. Ha Ha. We leave the club together at 10:30. Although the club has rules against dancers leaving the club with customers, they seem to accept we have a relationship and have never told me not to leave with him. After we go, we'll get a bite to eat and maybe a couple of drinks in a local club then call it a night. He always drops me off home about 12:00 or 1:00 a.m. and then goes home himself. As I said, he asks for very little in return, certainly no sex. I don't think he wants sex anyway, just companionship, in fact I think he's relieved by my no sex policy because it keeps him from cheating on his wife.

On Saturday nights, James takes me out on the town. Since I'm losing income by not being in the club dancing, he gives me the money I would have earned dancing in the Hot Zone. We eat at a lot of nice restaurants, go to movies occasionally, and then cap the night off in one of the many wine bars around Honolulu. It's really just a regular date. We've become quite the wine connoisseurs, or at least we're a few steps above drinking Thunderbird out of a paper bag on a street corner. He's even takes my Mom and her friends (all 70+) out to eat quite often. In essence, he's become a family member. I said we had a screwed up relationship. To make matters even nuttier, my Mom likes him even though she knows he's married. She thinks he's a stabilizing influence on me. If she only knew how crazy he was years ago as a young sailor running amok through the bars in the Philippines screwing every female he saw, more than 300 girls he says – whole bars including the mama sans. And you know what? I believe him. In the 1970's, Olongapo City in Subic Bay, Philippines was nothing but bars full of girls wanting to please the sailors from the nearby naval base and from ships that came into port. James said taking a girl home for the night, called an "overnight", cost about $20 and a quickie called a "short time" about $10. I still see signs of the wildness bred into him from that crazy environment from time to time, especially when he's had a few beers. I pride myself in being able to calm him down and he trusts me to do just that.

So do I trust him? Yes, I do. He knows more about me and my secrets than either of my husbands did. He has a set of keys to my apartment and I've even trusted him at various times with my credit cards and bank account. I have one of his credit cards to use whenever I need some money. Sounds like we're married doesn't it? Three years ago I trusted him to take care of me after I got my boob job. I've already told you about this earlier, but I think it bears repeating so you can get an idea of just how good a man he is. James drove me to the doctor and then took me to his home after the operation was finished. He took loving care of me, giving me pain medicine when I needed it, changed my bandages, gave me sponge baths and combed my hair while I bitched at him because of the pain. I slept on a couch in his bedroom because I had to be propped up in a halfway sitting position by pillows to be comfortable. I would call him in the middle of the night to take me to the bathroom and then give me more pain pills. I was a royal bitch and he said nothing, he just cared for me. For that, I will forever be thankful for him. And now, because of his help, I just graduated from college. He checked all of my homework especially the papers I wrote and helped me do the research for these papers. He says he did this because he wants me to be rich and successful so he can live off me when he gets old. I may just let him do that. By the way, this section on Sugar Daddies is much longer for a reason; James is helping me write it. But everything I said is true. I may even chose to have sex with him one day… Ha Ha…that's not true...Ha Ha. Suck it up James.

- Couples

Couples are a little difficult for me to judge or condemn. Although this pairing is mostly a man with a woman, now days, it can also include two women. Two men would be out of place in the Hot Zone…Ha Ha. Right now, for this specific discussion, I am just going to concentrate on the man/woman couple because this is far and away the most frequent types of couples I see. I'll address the woman/woman couple later. I don't mind dancing for couples of any type, if they're there for mutual arousal that will lead to wild sex later. One of the most profitable nights I had in the club was dancing for a young couple in our Champagne Room. The husband and wife each picked a dancer to take to up to the Champagne Room, the wife chose me. Ironically, the husband chose the dancer I described under Bitches earlier who had taken a severe disliking to me for some reason and wanted to beat me up when I first started dancing in the Hot Zone. Apparently she thought business was business and making money took priority over her dislike of me because we got along just fine for that short period of dancing for this couple. The wife bought me two bottles of champagne at $500 each, of which I shared 50/50 with the Hot Zone. She wanted me to accompanying them when they left the club for further partying and probably making love to me. I declined. I could see they were also going to buy drugs from the other dancer and I didn't really want to be part of that. But the good news was the $500 I made dancing for the couple and another $500 from dancing for other customers the rest of the night. I went home very happy.

I said I have no problem with couples as long as their enjoyment in watching me dance is for mutual stimulation. I do, however; object if the woman is there just to please her partner. I have to make a short speech of protest from my well worn soapbox if I see that. Ladies, why does your boyfriend or husband feel the need to come in here? Are your sex lives so screwed up that they need to come in here with you to get aroused? Do they get a charge out of watching you watch them lusting after naked girls. Don't you turn them on any more? If my boyfriend or husband insisted on coming in here even though I didn't, that would be a big neon lit message telling me I don't sexually arouse him anymore and maybe it's time for me to move on to someone I do turn on and who respects me. As a dancer, I see it every night, the woman with a sick grin on her face trying to be a good sport while her husband or boyfriend gets turned on by a dancer. SMACK HIM girls! Not that I'm bragging, but Hon, you just can't compete with us as far as sexual appeal. We're professionals. We keep our bodies in good shape and we're good at projecting sexuality. So what are you gaining by allowing him to drag you in here?

I've seen husbands and boyfriends grope their women as they watch me dance for them in the Table Dance room. Do they have fantasies it will turn me on watching them cavort and I'll say let's all go to hotel room and get it on? Sorry folks...that only happens in Penthouse magazine letters to the editor. If I ever came into this club with someone I thought I was having a relationship with and the moron started to grope me in public, I'm not sure how he'd be able to handle his drink after I'd broken all his fingers. Anyway, when the groping starts, that's my cue to put an end to the show and make a hasty exit. The last thing I need is to be arrested during raid.   The police here aren't very selective; they arrest and handcuff everyone then sort them out later. I already having an arrest on my record and would not fare well if I were arrested for a second time. Most of the time, the club employee watching over the Table Dance room puts an end to any groping sessions very quickly because he doesn't want to be caught a vice squad raid either and then fired by the club owner later by letting the groping happen in the first place.

- Foreigners

Well hell, as a Philippine national I'm a foreigner so I probably shouldn't be writing this but it's an appropriate subject since we get a lot of "other" foreigners in the Hot Zone. Right now, most of the foreigners we see are Japanese because Hawaii has been a popular tourist destination for them for several years. Over the last year; however, we've begun to see an influx of Chinese tourists. Both the Japanese and Chinese come to the Hot Zone in tourist groups, being driven here in a big bus or limousine with a guide showing them around and acting as a translator. It's good to know our club is included as a must see destination in someone's Michelin tourist guide for Honolulu. The groups are mostly comprised of men, naturally, but I swear to God I've also seen little old ladies. They must have thought they were taking the bus to one of our Buddhist temples....SURPRISE! For the most part, they're polite and well behaved. In fact, one of the biggest problems we have with them is they're too well behaved, or probably too shy, and hesitate to sit in front of any dancers. Maybe they just don't how to behave in a strip club. Usually, they cluster around one or two of the stages after their buying their beers and nervously ogle the girls. I think they're a little overwhelmed or embarrassed by it all but they never really seem to want to actually talk to a dancer or have her dance for them. This is hard to figure for the Japanese because they're famous for their sex vacations to other countries. For those foreign visitors who do want to have us dance for them, being good American hosts we naturally feel it's our duty to educate them on proper strip club etiquette. First lesson - "Filling the Garter." Since they're such honored guests, we tell them $20 bills in great quantities are the appropriate level of compensation for us to dance for them. For me, if they want to see my boobs and maybe my panties, it will take at least four or five $20 dollar bills, which I say is a greatly discounted price only for them. Want to see me naked? It's going to cost them at least five more. Second lesson - "Lady's Drinks." Lady's Drinks are only $40 and Special Lover's Drinks $60, all to be replenished frequently if they truly want our affections and want us to continue sitting with them. I've didn't tell you about Special Lover's Drinks earlier, it's a special offer we make only to our honored foreign guests. Like I said, we're really goodwill ambassadors. Third and final lesson - "Table Dance." If you want us to dance in the Table Dance room the price is $40 per song. And we tell them, if you take us to the Table Dance room "Me give you Good Love...cause Me So Horny"...Ha Ha. You must think we're terrible for doing this. OK, we are. This is mostly focused on the Japanese because they do bring a lot of money with them especially when the Yen is so strong against the dollar. They're actually getting off cheap compared to what they would be paying in the Ginza or Roppongi districts in Tokyo. And they get to sit with US!! I have no clue what the Chinese think about any of this. They are still very new at this. They come in, stare, and leave when their tour guide says to go. Very few speak English so they don't talk to us dancers, fewer still try and sit in front of us. Give them a few more years of tourism experience and U.S. cultural corruption and they'll soon be strong contributors to the yearly salary baseline of us dancers. Capitalism Baby!! I wonder what Chairman Mao would say about all of this. I don't know about all of the other girls, but I want to get ahead of the competition and start learning Chinese so I can at least convince them to pay me to dance in their own language. I wonder what's Chinese for "Want to buy me a Lady's drink"? (想要給我買夫人的飲料？) You are very handsome! (您是非常英俊的!). I am so horny (我是很有角的). The last one I had a little trouble with the term "horny". I was using a translation program I found on the Internet, so it might say I literally have horns. Ha Ha. All I can say is thank God for Internet translation software; however, sometimes the translations are not all that accurate, I've checked them against Tagalog and they don't do so good. I could have been saying in Chinese show me to the nearest Gay bar. Ha Ha.

- *Freeloaders*

Walk into the Hot Zone on any given night, or any strip club for that matter, and you'll see a crowd of men hanging around the edges of the stages usually right behind a customer that is paying a dancer. These are the Freeloaders and every dancer hates them, me in particular. Basically these idiots are trying to get a free ride watching the dancers get naked without actually paying the bus fare. This cheats us dancers out of income. Did I say I hate them? Getting naked for a paying customer is one thing and I've adjusted to that embarrassment over the years; however, being ogled by freeloaders standing behind him make me feel uncomfortable for some reason. It's like someone looking through your bedroom window watching you undress. It sounds nuts because we're in a strip club, but that's what it feels like. With a paying customer immediately in front of me, at least I can make believe we're in a one-on-one intimate situation, something not to be shared with a crowd of ogling idiots. I think my paying customers also feel the same way; at least they should, if I've done my job right. It's like someone saying something about his girlfriend. So I say to the Freeloaders….guys…STOP IT. What's wrong? Too shy to come and talk to me? Did you get tired of molesting your sisters and decide to have a night out. Make a commitment and decide to invest in having a good time, standing around ogling is not the way to do it. I've actually changed stages because of the Freeloaders clustering around the stage I was on. Every so often, one will have a twinge of conscience and actually stick some dollars in my garter but those events are few and far in between. Although I appreciate the gesture, I would rather they wait until I've finished with the customer I'm with and then come in front of me or go to another girl that doesn't have a customer. If you just want me to dance for you, come back when I'm free....oops, I mean available, I'm never free Ha Ha . You'll get your money's worth. I promise.

- Women Customers

Up until now, the customers I've described have all been men, which makes sense because it's men that mostly come into the Hot Zone. But surprisingly, women are coming into the club in increasing numbers either by themselves, with a significant other, or part of a group.

-- Women Alone

Although I mostly see women as part of a larger group of predominantly male customers or accompanied by a significant other, I do occasionally dance for women that came into the club by themselves. I don't think I would be far off characterizing these women as lesbians, or women who are testing themselves to see if they are lesbian by gauging their feelings about seeing a nude female. I've long since gotten over the uneasiness that both men and women feel when dealing with homosexuality. I see these women lonely customers who have the same right to sexual titillation as their straight male counterparts. If they like girls, so be it; in fact I've experimentally tried girls in the past, with a lot of alcohol involved, naturally. Although I found the experiences somewhat sexually stimulating, and I still like to see a well shaped punani, I didn't feel same level of arousal as I do with a man. Since I don't see anything particularly wrong with female homosexuality, I have no problem dancing for these single women. As I said earlier, money is money and I'm all about profit. I've never had one ask to buy me a Lady's drink but I'm sure that's coming as the women who come into the club become more comfortable with their sexuality. I'm just not sure how I'll respond. "More than likely, I'll say "sure, why not?" But that's a line I'll have to cross when the moment arrives. I'm sure my response will depend heavily on how I'm feeling at the time and how much alcohol I have in me Ha Ha. It would certainly be ground breaking for the club because I don't think I've seen any other dancer sit with a woman either. I guess it's a sign of the times. I wonder if my male stripper counterparts would feel comfortable dancing for other males, maybe if they're gay…I just don't know. I think this is a subject that would take rooms full of psychologists a lot of years to answer, and probably answer poorly. Me, I just know what I feel, and I honestly don't feel that it's wrong for a lesbian to enjoy herself. And truthfully, despite my earlier statement, if a woman asked to buy me a Lady's Drink, I would probably say yes.

- *Women as Part of a Larger Group*

As I said earlier, when I see women customers, they usually come in as part of a group of mostly men. Why they're part of the group is none of my business, co-workers? I often see that they are in over their heads and are trying to be good sports but are clearly uncomfortable about being in a strip club. If you're a man reading this book, think about you going into a male nude review with a group of women. Maybe that's a bad analogy, because perverted as men are, if they're straight, they'll ignore the penises flying around and concentrate on getting fucked by women who have been sexually aroused by those penises, or at least try to get a lot of cheap feels. Women are not as base as that and are usually just embarrassed. So what do they do when the men they came in with are staring at punanis? Like me, they may also look out of curiosity if anything, covertly, because they don't want their male friends to think they're lesbians. I think women are more comfortable flirting with homosexual feeling than men are. They'll make comments about a dancer occasionally to be one of the guys. Mostly, I think they wish they could be anywhere else in the world. I've had girls come from a larger group of men to sit in front of me, usually being egged on by the men. In these cases, I first wonder if she let herself be put in this position because she is wondering if she's a lesbian, but then I think "Crap, I've got another Show Off...this time the female version". And then I stand by for the outrageous behavior, which may be worse than what I receive from her male Show Off counterpart because being a female, she may think she can get away with more.

This makes me a little angry and not just from the standpoint of having yet another Show Off in front of me. No, I get angry because here's a fellow female, a sister, who feels she has to prove herself in front of her male friends or co-workers. If she's uncomfortable being in the Hot Zone she shouldn't be here and she clearly shouldn't be sitting in front of me to prove a point. This is all a lack of confidence. My rule of thumb when dealing with men is: I don't feel I have to prove myself to anyone or to get their approval. Fuck em. They need to deal with me on my terms and this poor girl sitting in front of me needs to bring her so called friends or male co-workers into line. She needs to grow a set of balls and tell them she's not going into a strip club with them. That's when I'll say, "You go, Girlfriend".

- Women Couples

Basically couples are couples and I was thinking about lumping them all together. But I decided to say a little something more about women couples. Having women couples come into the club is a phenomenon I've seen on the increase over the last few years. Unlike some of my fellow dancers, I don't mind dancing for girls but sometimes they are the customers I have the most problems with because as I said earlier, they don't seem to feel constrained by the no touching rules. These morons, and I hate to call my fellow sisters morons, don't realize, or worse, don't care that the no touching rules are for every customer, not just the men. They attempt all of the disrespectful actions that men try: sneaky touching, blowing on my punani, and rubbing dirty dollar bills all over my body; you name it, they've tried it. But with men, well let's say I can handle men. Usually if you give them a dirty look or snap at them a little, they get that "little boy being caught doing a bad thing" look and stop. Women act offended that I would take exception to their actions. I've had them continue to misbehave repeatedly after I've said I don't like it. Then they really get upset when I have the bouncers kick their sorry asses out of the club. Damn butch women. These are the types of customers I really worry will stay in the parking lot until the club closes and try to kick my ass when I come out. It hasn't happened yet, but it's a worry.

Working Outside the Club

I do quite a bit of escort and private party work outside the Hot Zone. Shhhh, don't tell anyone, this is another reason I'm concealing my identity in this book; I'll get fired if the Hot Zone management finds out about this. Of course they'll also have to fire two thirds of their dancers. We all do extra work, sometimes singularly or in groups. You can get your mind of out the gutter, I'm still not doing sex for money, I'm not a prostitute, remember? But there is still a lot of money out there without doing sex, it's a little slimier than dancing in the club but it's a lot of money and very hard to turn down. I can make more money in a couple of hours of freelancing than all night in the Hot Zone; I just have to swallow my morals a little bit more.

- *Escorting*

If you look in any phone book in any city, you'll see adds for escorts. Hawaii is no different, only I don't advertise in the phone book or anywhere else. A lot of the dancers in strip clubs and hostess bars do escorting side jobs. I just do it for customers I meet in the Hot Zone or by introduction via a current or previous customer. This is by far the easiest way for me to make a lot of money. I just go out on what for all intents and purposes is a date and get paid for it. I ask my "date" what role he'd like me to play and I do it. Does he want a girlfriend, fiancé, or wife? I can be that person. Or does he simply want company for a movie and eating in a nice restaurant? Again, here I am. My starting price is $500. That more than makes up for missing a night of work in the Hot

Zone. I only charge my Sugar Daddy $300 because he's safe and I enjoy his company. I already told you about going out with my Mr. Champagne Room customer. I've even gone with him to the mainland, as I do on occasion with my Sugar Daddy. I had another customer, a drug dealer I hate to say, that I would escort from time to time. How do I know he was a drug dealer? I saw him do it and it scared me every time I went out with him. He was nice enough, and he paid me a lot of money to hang all over him like a girlfriend, but he was living a very risky lifestyle and I had visions of being killed in a shootout or being picked by the police and deported. I don't escort him anymore, way too risky. As I wrote earlier, my dates with my Sugar Daddy only last until about 12:00 or 1:00 pm. One time, I talked him into taking me to all my dance club haunts and we didn't finish until the last club closed at 4:00 am. We ate breakfast after that and I don't think he got home until almost 6:00 am. I guess it was too much for his old body because he swore he would never do it again. Ha Ha. That's all right, just going out with him for a few hours on the weekend is enough because he does pay well and it gets me out of dancing in the Hot Zone.

- Private Dancing

Besides escorting, a lot of the dancers also do private dancing on the side. I do. Private dancing means bachelor parties, holiday parties where the participants have chipped in for naked girls, or one-on-one dancing for a customer in his home or a hotel room. How about being a naked sushi tray for a room full of Japanese businessmen? For some reason I get a lot of business during the Christmas season. I even have a special naughty elf outfit for the occasion. Nothing portrays the true spirit of Christmas like a naked elf giving lap dances. Ha Ha….Tis the season! Private dancing isn't illegal, at least not that I know about as long as the no touching rules are enforced. For the most part, it's done out in the open in clubs, etc., so if there are any illegalities everybody would know about it including the police. That's not to say it can't easily stray into illegal territory if the dancer or dancers don't keep strict control over their performance and the amount of touching they allow their customers. I insist on a minimum of $300 just for showing up to dance for an hour. The real money comes with the tips. On a good night, I can clear at least $600-$700 for a medium size party. Not bad for a couple hours of work. For security purposes, I usually try to go with one or two other girls who get paid the same. My routine is to strip naked first to show them my goods and provide a short show as I do every night in the Hot Zone. Then I dress and do lap dances for the rest of the time I'm there. Rule of Thumb when you do this kind of entertainment, ask for the money up front. It's harder to collect when you're ready to leave and everyone's drunk or they just want to cheat you out of your money. Up front is better when they're horny and anticipating your show. I usually feel I've gotten away with something when I can walk out of the party at the end of the night with money in hand and not being too badly mauled or arrested. As I said, I try to go with other girls for a reason; there are no real security enforcers during these private dances so I rely on safety in numbers. Of course I also rely on the good graces of the people hosting the party and on the party goers themselves. There's always the potential for ugliness after the party goers get drunk. I have to say I've never really been physically threatened although there have been times when I've left in a hurry after seeing a fight break out or after determining I would be in danger if I stayed any longer.

One thing that I do not allow is having my picture taken while I'm naked. It's not unusual for a customer to bring his camera to a party but I make sure to tell everyone up front no pictures. And that's not a hard rule to enforce because none of the married men at the party want their picture taken either or to be in any picture taken. Although I don't plan on being a movie star or run for political office where a scandalous naked picture could suddenly show up and embarrass you, I just don't want any nude pictures of me floating out in the digital world. I'm embarrassed enough by what I do out of necessity, I sure don't want it documented. Sometimes my ban on pictures causes a little heartburn, but they get over it soon enough. Men are men...and their small brains don't have long memory spans. Ha Ha.

Looking Forward

As I finish this book the end of another year is rapidly approaching and I've been dancing nude for nine years. NINE YEARS! To tell the truth, it's getting harder and harder to go into the Hot Zone and I'm not sure how much longer I'll be willing to do it. I hardly dance there anymore as it is. I now only go into the club when I need extra money. I found another job working in a resort hotel. The money is much less than what I make dancing but it feels cleaner and I look at the job as an investment in a career I will enjoy for the rest of my life. I like the hospitality business; I just need to keep grinding away at it. I've also started to take a language course to speak Mandarin Chinese. The Chinese will be the next foreigners to come to Hawaii in a big wave, like the Japanese did a few years ago, so I want to get ahead of the curve. Maybe I should just quit dancing cold turkey and burn my dancing outfits so I can't go back to dancing. Someday I will, but I'm not to that point yet. However, I've made the mental preparation to make that leap the very minute…better, the very second I'm financially able to. One thing that still hurts is the financial hole I dug during my last "breakout" when I opened a vegetable market. The credit card companies are still calling me on that one, or calling a phone number I used to have…Ha Ha. This is another reason for my desire for anonymity in this book. I DO have every intention in the world of paying them back but that will have to happen when I become more solvent. I just don't need calls from collection companies several times a day asking for money. Sometimes being an entrepreneur can be costly. Ha Ha.

My hotel job is the result of me getting my degree and then eliminating several forests sending out resumes. I picked a really bad time to try to find a legitimate job...right in the heart of a country-wide employment downturn. It's even worse in Hawaii...but I'm dealing with it. As I said, I've got tons of confidence and attitude...I'll succeed. I just hope I can hang in there working a 9-5 job, it's something I haven't done in a long time. It's a different routine and sometimes very tiring. For one thing, I'm not used to sleeping at night and then getting up and joining the rat race early in the morning. Ha Ha. Also, if I wanted to be very honest, which I have been in this book, I have to say I get tired working for "the man" too easily and quit. I'm just not prepared to "stick it out", "put in my time", etc., whatever you say. I'm more of an entrepreneurial person who would do better owning a business...again...maybe this time successfully. My goal is to become a millionaire when I'm 40, or failing that 50, or failing that.......150. Get my point? I AM going to eventually become a millionaire even if I die trying.

I do sometimes worry about the fallout of my long history of being a stripper as far as finding and keeping a normal job. Prior to me getting my current hotel job, I was really concerned about walking into a job interview only to see my interviewer was an old customer. The odds of that happening were pretty good considering how many men I've danced for over the years and how small Hawaii is. Now that I have a job, I scrutinize everyone I come into contact with to see if I recognize them as former Hot Club customers or if they recognize me. I hope if I do run into someone from my stripping life in the hotel, they won't remember me because I wear a conservative hotel uniform and look really respectable when I work here. I've heard a major factor in memory is the context in which that memory was made. In other words, if a Hot Zone customer does come in, he won't recognize me because his memory of me was formed in the Hot Zone where I'm wearing nothing or next to nothing. At least I hope it works that way. But if it doesn't, and I am recognized, I'll just have to brazen it out like I always do. I've been recognized out of the club before and the customer hasn't said anything because he doesn't want to admit he's been in a strip club, especially if he has his wife with him. Besides customers coming into the hotel, another major worry is being recognized as a stripper by a co-worker. It's happened before when I was selling cars, and it was a quite uncomfortable. In my new life now, it could open me up to all sorts of sexual blackmail. These are all things I should have considered when I first started to dance. But I was young and stupid and my immediate goal was just to pay my bills. I may have to move out of Hawaii eventually to get away from a history that could haunt me.

I hope this book's insider look at the stripping profession and the customers we service gives you a better understanding of how we live. As I thought about my fellow dancers while writing the book, I realized they're not so different from me. They may have arrived at the Hot Zone via different paths, but in the end, they all report to work every night, close their eyes (or maybe take a few stiff drinks), and proceed to get naked. My Thai friend said she came to work in the Hot Zone because it had the biggest advertisement in the phone book under night clubs. Ha Ha. And here she is, night after night, just like me. At the very least, I wanted you to understand we aren't the stereotypical strippers working a runway slowly taking our clothes off to a stripper anthem such as…... "*The Stripper*"….and kicking drunken sailors off the runway. DUH! Far from it. We're normal people, independent contractors if you will, trying to make a decent living in a dirty business. You could say we've sold our innocence and possibly our souls to make fast money and you might be right. I can definitely tell that my soul has taken a pounding. But it hasn't completely deserted me, nor will it. Maybe my Catholic upbringing armored it even though I vary rarely go to Mass. As I said earlier, I jealously guard the little shreds of dignity I still retain. I refused to become hooker. I came close once, when I really needed the money and one of my steady Hot Zone customers was willing to pay me to have sex with him. I said yes, and got all the way to the foyer of the hotel he had rented a room in only to have a conscience attack and quickly leave the hotel. I vowed to myself I would rather be homeless than to go down the sex for hire road. I have never looked back.

Earlier in the book, I talked about having a boyfriend but I've since kicked him to the curb. I could see very clearly he was going to be future ex-husband number three and I don't need that grief. I have a new boyfriend now but I don't think I have a future with him either. That doesn't bode well for my ability to have any kind of a meaningful relationship. I think that's a casualty of my being a stripper where I've lost faith in men in general. I'm hoping having a normal job will remedy that by bringing me into contact with more normal men, men I will be willing to consider as a mate and father of my children. But not now…not now. Damn it.

I am still friends with my Sugar Daddy. He is a connection to my stripping life that may be hard to break because we've developed into good friends. He makes me laugh and he does provide money to help me make ends meet. But we have no future together and he understands. I would marry him in a minute, however, if he became free because he's so good to me, but that's not in the cards. Maybe in the next life. He does say that if I do get involved with someone, that guy better brings some spurs and a saddle because I'll be a hard ride and a bitch to break…Ha Ha. For right now, my theme song is pretty much *"Alone Again…Naturally."* So, I keep marching on…still dancing occasionally, still doing a private show occasionally, but looking for any opportunity to make that final break out of the sex trade. Maybe if I can sell enough copies of this book, I'll have enough financial breathing room to make a final break from stripping. So please customers, invest in my future. Get another stripper off the runway and into the normal rat race of life...…Ha Ha. This might fall under the category of be careful what you ask for…Ha Ha.

Oh, as one last thought, I still haven't had full on sex with my Sugar Daddy…maybe I should as a reward for several years of faithful service. I did promise we would have hot, sweaty monkey sex if we sell this book…so he's praying it's a success. Again, he wrote that….QUIT BEGGING JAMES, Ha Ha.

End of Course Test

I know I've rambled a lot in this book but I tried to keep it focused on a few major themes and I hope I was as least consistent in my discussions of these themes. But, if I lost some of my consistency, so what? Life is full of inconsistencies and often my views on any given subject might change from day to day or year to year depending on my feelings at the time. I don't know how many times I wrote and then rewrote sections of this book because I changed my mind about things. If I'm depressed, my thoughts and views are a little negative; if I'm happy, just the opposite. If I have PMS, they're completely hostile to everything including myself...Ha Ha. Aren't most people this way? Anyway, I thought I would end my story by summarizing some of my observations on men and on men-women relationships based on my years of observing people while I danced. I think my perspective on the human condition is unique in that being a stripper has allowed me to see the darker side of humanity. In the remainder of this book, I'm going to ask a few questions for you to examine your own feelings not only on relationship issues but a number of other topics to see how they compare to mine. I realize I'm still young in comparison to most of you, having just turned 31 and you probably don't think I have the chops to offer any kind of observations on life. I think; however, the hard miles over rough road that years of nude dancing have put on my soul have matured me well beyond my physical years. Well, matured me with respect to full blown cynicism of life in the underbelly of polite society. I've certainly crammed a lot of "been there and done that" living into my few years of existence. So if my questions and my observations behind those questions seem a little skewed or cynical, they probably are. But I won't apologize because I generally have good reasons for my opinions which were often formed based on bitter experience. I sometimes wish that my life had been more normal, like the lives of my high school friends who all have husbands and children. Nah…not really. I think their lives are boring. I've tried it before…the result? Two ex-husbands and a bunch of other relationship mistakes. So what do I know, what does anyone really know? Anyway…let's begin…...

Stripping

You should have guessed this was going to be my first subject, after all this is what the book is about and I've expended a lot of effort describing the profession and telling you how I got into it. I hope none of you squirm when I call it a profession. I've done it several times in the book because I think it is. Just getting naked is not enough. There are certain appearance criteria you have to meet as well as basic job skills to master before you can be successful…just like any profession. I don't think I'm exaggerating this just to make myself and my fellow strippers seem more acceptable and legitimate. We are legitimate and participants in a profession that's been around for a long time. I asked you earlier to look up Salome. Did you read about her "dance of the seven veils"? We strippers have a long and rich history.

As I wrote earlier, money was a part of my decision to be a dancer, but not all. I could have found an alternative way to make a living but I didn't because of the phenomenal money you can make stripping. And I started stripping only because I badly needed that money. There is; however, a significant downside - loss of self esteem and a total loss of faith in mankind. It drains you morally. I described how various dancers, myself included, fortify themselves before dancing (or while dancing) either through drinking or taking drugs. It's no mystery why they feel the need to do this. So….

Question 1. I guess this goes right to the heart of this book…Could you ever be a stripper? Have you ever considered it? It should have been obvious I was going to ask these questions. I'll bet these same questions were running through your mind as you were reading my story. So…could you be a stripper? Could you get naked in public? No? **Are there any circumstances that would make you change your mind**? Understand, I'm directing these questions at those ladies who have now, or had when they were younger, the requisite good looks and good body that would actually allow them to be a successful stripper. If you weren't blessed with beauty or at least a good body, then this question is moot. That's a cruel statement but realistic. As I wrote, my decision to be a stripper was not all that traumatic for me. I needed money; wanted independence from my mother; and I had a friend convince me to try it, actually holding my hand when I started. Although I faced my first customer with a little trepidation, I wasn't by any means a sheltered virgin, so I got over the trauma of taking my clothes off in front of a stranger in a crowded club rather quickly. I have to admit having him stuff money into my garter was certainly encouraging and going home that first night with more money than I'd ever seen in my life was even more encouraging. The money aside, I just didn't seem to be largely inhibited about being naked. I had a good body and no problem showing it off. Maybe you can make a good case of me being young and stupid. What about you? Could you do the same thing? Come on Ladies, haven't you ever wondered about the freedom of sexually enticing someone? Or about actually walking out on a stage and teasing a bunch of men? Just close your eyes and imagine yourself doing something this daring. Imagine the power of having a bunch of men in the palm of your hand. Try practicing a strip routine in the privacy of your bedroom. Or better yet, try it for your husband. You might be surprised at his response. Break out of your shyness, drop the blanket and show him what you got. I'll bet he fantasizes a lot about that. Or are you a little sexually repressed? All I can say is don't criticize the profession of stripping from a moral high ground if you haven't tried it, or visited a strip club…or going further, talked to a stripper. You might find they're not much different than you or weren't much different than you when they started.

Question 1A. This is a short extension of the first question. When I first began my stripping career, I found myself having to decide if I was willing to do a little more than just taking my clothes off if I wanted to compete with the other dancers. Although my first club specified a "no touch" policy, it was readily apparent the club management would turn a blind eye to dancers allowing a little touching in a private booth or in a separate champagne room. It was not only allowed but unofficially encouraged. So my question is, **if you were a dancer, would you be willing to go the "extra mile" to be able to compete with fellow dancers?** In other words would you allow some wandering hands or be willing to do lap dances? I allowed it to a certain extent because of the money and because I was young and stupid. I got busted for my efforts too and now I have a criminal record. I was just lucky I didn't get deported. Would I do it again knowing what I know now? NO.

Question 1B. This question is for everyone. **How do you view me and my fellow dancers because we take our clothes off for a living?** I realize your answers may be partially (or painfully?) rooted in how religious you are, but I'd appreciate an honest answer. Of course, if you are painfully religious, you probably wouldn't be reading my book in the first place...Ha Ha. **Would you look down on us or treat us with contempt if we were to meet you and you were aware of our occupation?** I guess the real acid test question is "**Would you let us date your sons**"? Ha Ha. If you said "No" to dating your sons, or you would feel some contempt, I'll respect that answer but not without a little sadness. One of my goals in writing this book was to explain our lives in terms of how we're normal people caught up in a profession that's not socially accepted. I was trying to break the popular (and mostly wrong) stereotype of strippers. I emphasized several times that to us dancers, stripping was just a job we had to support our families and to keep a roof over our heads. Stripping is also a means to an end for a lot of the dancers, taking the good looks and bodies that God gave us and using them to provide us a short period of high income to help prepare for later in life. For example, a lot of dancers are college students using their stripping money for tuition. I don't think being a stripper represents any kind of deviant sexual behavior, just a means to an end. I don't really recall any dancers I've worked with that I could label as a sexual deviant. Indeed they are some of the most sexually normal people I know; certainly more normal than a lot of customers we dance for.

Question 1C. Now let me put a little further twist on my basic question. If you said you feel some contempt for us because we are strippers, how do you feel about the people that come into the club to watch us? As I related in my book, I've see a wide variety of customers who come into the Hot Zone for a lot of different reasons. One, being simply to see naked women. Other reasons are not so simple. A lot of our customers just want to talk to someone, to have a neutral third party sounding board that will listen to their complaints about home or work without being judgmental. I don't often have much good advice to give other than being commiserating and encouraging. Maybe that's enough because it's more than what they're obviously getting elsewhere…like at home? I strongly believe the married men I see should be sharing the same conversation they have with me with their wives or significant others. Ladies, this is you I'm talking about. Some of your husbands may be my best customers. How do you feel about that? If your husbands are sitting in front of me, you need to look for shortfalls your home life. What's missing? I talk to them because I want to keep them as customers; you should talk to them because you love them....period. It's very obvious they love you. I can tell that by the way they light up when they talk about you and their children, but the intimate things some of them say should stay in the home. Your family dynamic would be much stronger if you were able to effectively talk to each other....about anything. I can communicate with my customers because I only have a business relationship with them, a short one based solely on how much money they're willing to stick in my garter. I'm not judgmental or biased in any way. Does your love for each other as a couple constrict the freedom of discussion? Are there taboo areas you're afraid to discuss, but really should? Think about it. You can call me in the morning...and I will send my consultation bill to you in the mail....Ha Ha.

Question 1D. For the men. **Would you have any pre-determined prejudices if you met someone you knew was a stripper or used to be a stripper?** I think the fear most of us dancers have is men who know we are (or were) strippers expecting sexual favors from us because "that is what we do." This would make it very hard for us to migrate from the dance floor into a normal work environment. Would we get any respect as a fellow professional given our background? Would we be especially vulnerable to sexual harassment and possibly to blackmail if a male co-worker were to tell us that he'll spread the word of our stripper past to everyone if we didn't have sex with him. It certainly wouldn't make a healthy work environment and I am not sure we would be defended by our fellow co-workers or management…...because after all, we got naked for a living. In fact, the management might want to know why our past life as a stripper didn't come up during the job interview process. Good question, and naturally a charge we can't defend ourselves against. Our stripper lives didn't come up during the job interview because we hid them….DUH! Besides, I just can't imagine how the subject of me being a stripper would be inserted into any answer I gave to a job interview panel. For example…Question…"what previous job experiences do you think may be of benefit to this company"? Do you absolutely think I would say: "Well, I got naked a lot and got paid a lot of money doing it, so I know how to manage money and talk customers into spending their hard earned money on me?" Sometimes I think our fear about being exposed as strippers in a normal work environment might be a little baseless. A lot of the money we got was based on tips from customers and under-the-table payments from the clubs so hiding our past isn't that difficult unless you got arrested like I did. And, I've seen this quite often, men that I recognize dancing for don't recognize me because they saw me in the context of the dark lighting of a strip club and I don't look the same during the day. Sounds dumb, but it's true.

Often if the context is different or missing, perception and recognition are likewise missing.

Question 2. All of these questions are for the women. Have you ever been in a strip club where women get naked or even partially undressed? I guess there are a number of aspects to this question. First, **do you, or do you think you would, like to see other women naked**? As I wrote before, I like to see naked women. I think they're beautiful, and I admit it, I do get a sexual reaction to a beautiful naked female body. That doesn't mean I'm a lesbian, far from it, I'm totally into men. However, I might be a little bi-sexual and I probably wouldn't mind a ménage à trois under the right circumstances and with a liberal application of alcohol of course. Ha Ha. I did experiment with women once or twice when I was younger, but nothing serious, just enough to realize that it had to be men in my future. For those of you ladies who have been in strip club with naked women, how did you feel? Embarrassed, turned on, or just felt out of place? I often see a "what am I doing here" look on women that come into the Hot Zone with a larger group of mostly men. First, let me say I think it's inconsiderate of the men to even come into the club when they know they have women with them. They shouldn't be forcing the women to be "one of the guys." Or try badly to be one of the guys. It's embarrassing for everyone and will eventually result in a poor workplace environment. Ladies, if you are uncomfortable, don't be afraid to walk out of the club, or to even say right from the start I'm just not going to go in there. Real stand up guys would realize their mistake right away and go to a place where everyone is comfortable. I'm just wondering how these same guys would react in a male nude review where nude men are dancing and there's a lot of big weenies flying around. Then Ladies, you can dare your fellow male co-workers to put a dollar in a male dancer's g-string with his teeth. Of course you would have to take pictures of that for future reference. Just saying…...

Question 2A. Would you go into a strip club to watch naked women with your husband or boyfriend? I think I may have been a little harsh on this subject earlier in the book. My thought process was that if your husband or boyfriend wants to see naked women over your objections then your relationship might be in trouble because I don't think you are a sufficient turn on for him. In the short term, you might benefit from this because you'll get a lot of good sex out of your aroused man, but is he really making love to you or the naked strippers he ogled? In the long term, your relationship is in trouble. God help you if the dancer you're watching catches wind that there is even the slightest rift between you and your man with respect to being in the club. Sometimes when a dancer sees this she will become a complete bitch and try to drive a greater wedge between the both of you by flirting with him, leaving you to stew in jealousy. Hey, I've done this in the past when I totally disliked the couple. So, I'm a bitch!

HOWEVER, if you are there as a consenting couple for mutual arousal, kind of like watching a porno movie together, then by all means knock yourselves out. Go into the club, drink, get aroused and then go home and fuck your brains out; sounds kind of poetic. I don't mind dancing for this type of a couple. In fact, I enjoy watching their reactions as I push their buttons. I've even been known to stretch the legal boundaries to help these couples reach even greater sexual heights. Occasionally, I've even been caught up in the sexual heat of the situation which led to me trying even harder to spike their sexual tension. No, I've never gone home with a couple....sorry Penthouse.

Question 2B. What about in a Male Review where men get naked?

Have you ever gone into a club to watch men strip naked? Male reviews are not as common as strip clubs featuring women, but they're out there. I attended one once and had a great time. A lot of fun putting my money into someone else's garter for a change, in this case it was a well filled out g-string the dancer had on, a last piece of clothing that was soon quickly removed. I have to admit the dancers looked good......very good......very, very good. Ha Ha. Some of them would have split me in half if I was foolish enough to have sex with them. I had fun, my girlfriends had fun, as did every other woman in the club. But as I said earlier, the environment of this club in no way compared to the environment I work in nightly. In male-oriented clubs such as the Hot Zone, the fun is noticeably reduced in favor of lust - hungry, primitive lust.

Men

You probably could have also guessed I'd ask questions about men because they've definitely influenced my life and in a few cases bent my life's path all to hell. I think this is the category where I'll admit my views are all skewed. After all, I work in a profession where I don't exactly see the best side of men. I also go out to normal night clubs a lot after work to meet and talk to normal men but I have to say, from what I've seen of the newer generation of men in these clubs, I'm not sure they're all that different than the men I see in the Hot Zone. What happened to gentlemen? What happened to men you can have a good conversation with? And the big question, what happened to men who would be good husbands?

Frankly, as a woman, I have conflicted feelings regarding men and I don't think I'm alone in womanhood with these feelings. Men often say women confuse them, well, Dude, it's the same with us women. We're totally confused by men and their actions most of the time. The problem is, if you're not a lesbian, you need men for sexual satisfaction if nothing else. You notice I didn't say we need men for financial support and protection. We don't. I've been doing a fine job surviving (and even thriving) without a consistent male presence in my life. Relying too much on men leaves you vulnerable. Why does a women stay with a man even if he abuses her? Answer: She's often totally dependent on him for food and shelter and she has nowhere else to go or the necessary skills to take care of herself. But sex on the other hand is a different thing. Yes, we're not in the Puritan age so we (I) can admit to having sexual urges and there's nothing more satisfying on this earth that having a good sexual encounter with a handsome young stud.   Don't get me wrong, masturbation is a great substitute, I often let my fingers do the walking but I'll take a willing young man anytime to quench my sexual urges.   There's just no substitute for the real thing. But here's where the rub comes in. A lot of men, particularly young men, suck at sex. Foreplay is a lost art. Oral sex is often the lesser of the skills a young man will bring to bed, if he has any skills at all. He'll be enthusiastic, sure, but being from the video game generation, he'll have very little patience with spending even a short amount of time orally lavishing our clits, expecting us to have a thunderous climax within one or two licks.   And young men also seem to think fucking is a speed sprint with the winner being whoever finishes first.   But these sexual shortcomings in young men are all fixable with the right teacher...and with patience......a lot of patience. Ha Ha. However, this leads me to another problem I have with men, their need to own and dominate. Having read my book, you should know by now I'm the last person on this earth a man should try to dominate. I'm very poor at submitting to the will of anyone else. In fact I suck at it...which maybe is why I've been married twice. But this dominance/subservience problem always arises when you give in and have sex with a man, he now thinks he owns you or has a significant say in how you lead your life. For all you male readers, this is totally nuts, not only for me but I hope for all of my sisters. We all have the same right of self determination as you do sex or no sex. You may offer advice, and I do like to get advice, but don't expect me to say yes sir and march on, and don't be hurt if I chose my own path after receiving your advice. Finally, to complete my bitch session, Ladies, have you ever tried to have a conversation with a man, especially a young man. Does it ever rise above "Where's my beer" or "I'm horny"? I see this all the time dancing when I try to talk to a customer. It seems very hard for them to respond coherently with their little brain dominating their thought processes. Ha Ha.

So here's a couple of test questions. Feel free to cheat and browse what I've written earlier in the book or reread what I just ranted about. Ha Ha.

Question 3. If a young man approaches you in a nightclub and asks to buy you a drink, how do you respond? If he's a handsome man and you say yes would you then feel obligated to do anything else with him based on that drink? My response? As I wrote earlier, I don't often accept offers to buy me a drink because if I say yes, the man buying the drink now thinks I'm obligated to him. Not! I feel absolutely no obligation at all from having accepted a drink. If I let someone buy me a drink I'm just allowing him to audition for further attention from me. If he fails the audition, then I have no problem walking away with a polite thank you. Buying me the drink was his initiative, not mine. Sometimes, if I'm feeling like a Bitch, I'll let someone whom I know upfront won't pass my audition, buy me a drink anyway…along with a drink for friends who came into the club with me. If he's smart, he's going to see this as a rejection and quickly walk away because he can see I'm being a bitch. If he's dense, he'll keep buying drinks to impress us and when he runs out of money, we'll thank him and say goodbye. B I T C H E S. We know it, and that's definitely what he's thinking. If I let a promising young men buy me a drink and he does pass my initial audition and I may "let him" talk me into dinner. Even then I still will not feel any obligation for sex. To put it succinctly, I will have sex when I feel like having sex and it will be on my terms. My decision to sleep with someone is based on a number of factors, not just a drink or dinner. I firmly believe that I have to experience some chemistry with him and I have to think there may be some promise in a relationship before I even consider sex. I know what you're thinking based on reading my book. You want to ask "how is that approach working out for you? Have you had any successes with relationships"? My response is Bite me; at least my intentions are good. I will eventually find a lifetime partner, but in the meantime, I'm not giving my pussy away to any young stud that walks by. I put my punani on display for all to see every night, so I strongly reserve the right to when and where I use it.

Question 3A. Regardless of what I said above about needing to see some promise in a relationship before I commit to sex, I admit it there have been exceptions where I've been just plain horny and have lowered my standards a little (a lot actually…Ha Ha). To my credit this doesn't happen often, but it happens. For example, I had sex one day with a guy I picked up while standing in line to get a cup of coffee at Starbucks. It was a mistake because the sex wasn't that satisfying, but I had this urge (yes women get urges) and he was an available and reasonably handsome young man. **So my question is, how do you feel about casual sex?** Have you ever had sex because you were horny and just wanted to have sex? No love involved, just scratching an itch. That's a feeling societies have traditionally frowned upon with respect to their women. Women are not supposed to get horny. Men are expected to be horny and women compliant. Dude, I am anything but compliant. Hah. Want to confirm that women get horny? Go to a male strip show and see how NOT horny the women in the audience are.

Question 3B. Would you ever buy a guy a drink? Have you ever wanted to buy a guy a drink but wondered what the consequences would be? I'll bet a lot of you Ladies would never consider being so forward, at least some of you older ladies. My response? Hell yes, and I've done it. And being even more forward, I've even ask men to dance in a nightclub. Again, it all depends on the mood I'm in and whether or not I feel attraction for a guy. You can bet I had an ulterior motive (SEX), just like a guy who buys a woman a drink. But as a woman, I can be much more successful than a guy with respect to finding a bed partner for the night. I have the pussy, so as a woman I can bat 1,000 in picking up someone. I think I saw a t-shirt once that read "I have the pussy, so I make the rules." Guys any debate about that? I'm sorry your batting average is always going to be much lower. It's good to be a girl! Ha Ha. So I reiterate, why not take a chance and be a little bit forward. I've said often enough men are stupid and need to be led around by the nose or some other piece of their anatomy. So Ladies, take the initiative if you are lonely and tired of waiting for a man to step up to the plate. Besides you may not like the man that does approach you so why not pick out someone you do fancy or lust for?

Question 4. If you are in a relationship, should you allow the man to control every aspect of your life? I could also re-phrase this question to read should you allow your significant other to control every aspect of your life? My response is not only NO! but HELL, NO! Ladies, don't ever turn over total control of your life to someone else. What happens if your relationship goes south and you're left flat footed with nothing and no idea of how to take care of yourself? Relationships are about sharing, not domination. I don't mind sharing my life but I really insist of controlling my own life. I haven't struggled to make a living all these years and put myself through college just to hand some guy the keys to my life and say here "Drive it." Some guys may object to that and may even feel threatened by an independent minded woman such as me. That guy will never have a relationship with me. I don't like men who lack such self confidence they feel uncomfortable with my independence. Trying to dominate is the sign of a weak man. I want a partner, not a master. On the positive side, I will never be rejected by a man for being a "clinger." Ha Ha.

Question 5. Do you even believe in marriage?

I guess I need to ask this question it's a very basic relationship decision that couples eventually have to face. Some people decide to get married relatively early in a relationship, while others wait for years before making the plunge or deciding to move on. In all honesty I can't say I don't believe in marriage because damn it, I've been married twice which is pretty blasphemic for a Catholic girl. I'm pretty sure I felt love towards both my husbands, but in retrospect as I've been writing this book, I'm wondering if I used both to escape from difficulties that were going on in my life at the time. With my first husband, I wanted to get out from under my oppressive mother, and for my second husband, I wanted an escape from stripping. Maybe why that's why both marriages ultimately failed, they were for the wrong reasons and had no solid foundation of a strong love or even a friendship that would have enabled us to survive the rigors that everyone faces in marriage. That and the lack of a willingness to compromise which couples in love are fully willing to do to accommodate the wishes of their significant other to make their marriage work. Me? I'm not even sure I want to marry again. My last two experiences have convinced me I'm not cut out for marriage. Besides, I just found this statistic on the Internet: "...the divorce rate in America for first marriage is 41%; the divorce rate in America for second marriage is 60%; the divorce rate in America for third marriage is 73%. Hmmm, so I'm wondering what my chances are for happiness in a third marriage. It doesn't look promising. Yet, I'm still looking. I'm probably an idiot, but deep down inside, I think I still desire a lifelong mate...or maybe a better word is partner.

So that gets me to my basic question, do you think being married is necessary in today's society? Fifty years ago, the answer would have been yes if you wanted to have children, because you were a social outcast if you had children (and God forbid had sex) outside of marriage. Today? Women are independent and, I think, can have a fulfilling life without the benefit of a man. Well, other than sex...but that can be rented as needed with no strings attached...Ha Ha.

The Sex Industry in General

Since you're all in a sexual frame of mind, I wanted to do an informal survey regarding how you feel about the sex industry in general. In Hawaii, we have a thriving sex industry partially because of our tourist trade and also because of a strong Asian influence. Bargirls that keep company with paying customers and even go home with them for money are an accepted part of the culture in many Asian countries. Having a daughter or daughters as bar girls can be a major source of income for a poor family that keeps food on their table and a roof over their head. The customer I call my Sugar Daddy in the book was stationed in Subic Bay for several years during the 70' and 80's. The bar girl industry was in strong swing both in Subic Bay and Clark AB back then. In fact it was one of the major ways for girls to meet and marry U.S. Servicemen. My friend saw nothing wrong with this and neither did the Filipinos. It was viewed as a major means for these girls and their families to break out of grinding poverty they lived in. I think I would have been one of the girls working in a club if I had been alive back then. But my point is, that same acceptance of the bar girl culture is here in Hawaii. Although I'm not advocating a sex industry for the U.S. like they had in the Philippines in the 70's and 80's, some of the girls were even sold to the clubs by their parents, I am thinking that there can be a legitimate place for some sort of a regulated sex trade - if for nothing else than to keep the customers and girls safe. You will always have some type of sexual services bought and sold; the profession is as old as time itself. Often these services are at the peril of both buyer and seller, so why not regulate it? There are many countries in the world that do just that. Go to Australia or a number of European countries. You will see brothels advertised in their newspapers and phone books. Check out punter websites on the Internet.

Question 6. Would you be in favor of legalized prostitution?

As I wrote earlier, I don't like having prostitutes on the street here in Honolulu. It's a sad and dangerous life for them and I think they would be better off working in Hostess bar or stripping. On the street, they're at the mercy of both the police and their pimps. That said, I really wouldn't have a problem with the prostitutes if they were an acknowledged profession by the state and city governments thereby gaining some level of legal acceptance which would result in a better working environment for them and safety for their customers. I fail to understand the problem the U.S. has with legalized prostitution. A lot of countries accept it, and therefore gain a level of control over it. Having a legal sexual outlet would probably get a lot of would be sex offenders off the street, certainly a threat I look out for every night. What are your thoughts? I know if you're from the Midwest Bible Belt with a strong religious background, your answer is going to be a resounding no. But I would hope you would take an unbiased look at the subject, both the pros and the cons instead of a rote religious response, and give me your **considered** answer. Some sort of a sex industry is always going to be around, even in the middle of Iowa, it just a matter of making it safe and supervised. Legalizing it would take all of the pimps and associated crime pretty much out of the picture and importantly, give men an outlet to release their sexual tension. There is one caution I must mention to this. I'm only talking about voluntary participation in the sex trade; not sexual slavery that can be prevalent in poor countries. I absolutely do not agree in the trafficking of persons for sexual purposes (i.e. kidnapping young girls and forcing them into prostitution).

Question 7. Would you accept Hostess Bars in your town?

This is not a hard issue for me. Hostess bars are part of the Filipino culture as much as they are in a number of Asian countries. I live close to a number of hostess bars now and don't see any problems. Maybe it's cultural. I do think having a place for lonely men to go to talk to a woman has a lot of benefits, certainly more than any negative issues you can come up with. I think there something fundamentally therapeutic about the whole concept of a hostess bar. And if there are after hours dates arranged, with sex as a possibility (God forbid), then so what? Can't that also be called a normal date? You know, I think the whole concept of men meeting women over the Internet is a little too impersonal. Everybody looks great on the Internet or you need to look great by any means available. So sometimes it's a buyer beware social environment. There are no such surprises in hostess bars. You go in, buy a girl a drink and talk. And if you like what you hear and see, you can take it from there. Or if you go in just to have someone to talk to, to decompress from whatever problem that's bothering you, how can a hostess bar be wrong in providing you that venue? All I can say is hostess bars are an Asian phenomenon that you can find in Hawaii and California. Maybe the concept should be exported into other U.S. cities. It might cut down on the social crimes.

End of Course

I'd like to thank you for putting up with me and my life's story. I don't know what you got out of my story, but it was certainly very therapeutic for me. Maybe I need to talk my issues out with a hostess bar girl. Ha Ha. Did you object to any of my questions? I was hoping they would take you out of your normal day-to-day life and consider issues other people face routinely. We can't all be housewives in the Midwest, sheltered from problems that face big city dwellers. We weren't all born rich. Most of us have to scramble to make it from day to day. Sometimes the choices we make to survive are unfortunate, but there you have it. We do the best we can even if we're in objectionable circumstances. That's me. I will not always be a stripper. It was a means to an end – to be able to eat and pay the rent…period. I certainly won't be doing it for much longer. I will miss the big paydays but I think it's time to move on under my own terms, not when the club owner says don't bother to come back. I wish you all the best of luck in whatever you do. Just think about me laboring away in a 9-5 job in Hawaii if someone finally likes my resume.

Thank you……

Love, Amaya

www.ingramcontent.com/pod-product-compliance
Lightning Source LLC
Chambersburg PA
CBHW060451290526
45791CB00001B/67

* 9 7 8 1 4 9 4 7 5 4 6 0 0 *